Yiddish

AND

English

T0288349

Sol Steinmetz

Yiddish

AND

English

The Story of Yiddish in America

Second Edition

The University of Alabama Press
Tuscaloosa

Copyright © 1986, 2001
The University of Alabama Press
Tuscaloosa, Alabama 35487-0380
All rights reserved
First edition published 1986. Second edition 2001.
Manufactured in the United States of America

9 8 7 6 5 4 3 2 1
10 09 08 07 06 05 04 03 02

The paper on which this book is printed meets the minimum
requirements of American National Standard for Information
Science-Permanence of Paper for Printed Library Materials,
ANSI Z39.48-1984.

Library of Congress Cataloging-in-Publication Data

Steinmetz, Sol.
    Yiddish and English : the story of Yiddish in America / Sol Stein-
metz—2nd ed.
        p. cm.
    Originally published: University, Ala. : University of Alabama
Press, ©1986. With additional material.
    Includes bibiographical references and index.
    ISBN 0-8173-1103-3 (pbk. : alk. paper)

    1. Yiddish language—United States. 2. Yiddish language—Foreign
words and phrases—English. 3. English language—Foreign words
and phrases—Yiddish. 4. Jews—United States—Languages. I. Title.

PJ5119.U5 S74 2001
439'.1'0973—dc21

                                        2001017106

British Library Cataloguing-in-Publication Data available

To Tzipora

Contents

Preface

This is an updated edition of the book published in 1986 under the title *Yiddish and English: A Century of Yiddish in America.* Much has happened in the world since its publication, including the end of the Cold War and the opening of cyberspace. These global events have had significant impact on the use of languages, and the Yiddish language is no exception. The dissolution of the Soviet Union triggered the mass emigration of Soviet Jews, many of them Yiddish speakers, to countries like Israel and the United States. In turn, the wide dissemination of information through the Internet has facilitated global communication among thousands of Yiddish students, scholars, writers, and editors. The resulting infusion of new blood into the field of Yiddish study and scholarship has revitalized interest in a language that has often been regarded as moribund. This latest revival of interest in Yiddish is described in Chapter 3, "Yiddish in the United States."

As Yiddish on the American scene is now well past the century mark, it seemed appropriate to change the subtitle of this revised edition from "A Century of Yiddish in America" to the more encompassing "The Story of Yiddish in America." Indeed, in the process of revising the book, the author came to realize that the story of Yiddish is still evolving, transcending rather than being circumscribed by time.

Acknowledgments

I wish to express my deep appreciation to the following individuals who read parts of this book at various stages of its writing and gave me the benefit of their criticism and suggestions: Clarence L. Barnhart, dean of American lexicographers, to who I am especially grateful for allowing me free use of his great file of citations; Robert K. Barnhart, my long-time associate, editor of the *World Book Dictionary* and many other outstanding reference books; Lillian Mermin Feinsilver, noted editor and writer, author of *The Taste of Yiddish,* to whose work on the influence of Yiddish on English I am greatly indebted; Robert A. Fowkes, professor emeritus of Germanic Linguistics at New York University; Reason A. Goodwin, linguist and editor, author of the *Troika* introduction to Russian and other scholarly works; Joseph C. Landis, professor of English at Queens College, editor of the literary quarterly *YIDDISH;* and Nathan Süsskind, professor emeritus of German at City College of New York and an authority in Yiddish linguistics.

I also extend special thanks for their help and encouragement to John Algeo, professor of English at the University of Georgia and former editor of *American Speech;* I. Willis Russell, professor emeritus of English at The University of Alabama; Dina Abramowicz, librarian of the YIVO Institute for

Jewish Research; and Rose Zaiman, of the World Jewish Congress. In addition I wish to thank Malcolm M. MacDonald, director of The University of Alabama Press, for his special interest in this book, and the members of his outstanding staff; Cynthia Dessen, who copyedited the manuscript; my colleagues at Barnhart Books—Shirley Abramson, Cynthia A. Barnhart, Anne-Luise Bartling, Carol G. Braham, Albert S. Crocco, and Richard D. Whittemore; and Evelyn Bogner, reference librarian at the New Rochelle, New York, Public Library.

I also take this opportunity to thank my wife, Tzipora Mandel Steinmetz, our children, Jacob and Deborah, Abraham and Erica, Steven and Liba, and my mother, Lea Zweibel Steinmetz, for the unfailing support they have given me and my work through the years.

Finally I wish to acknowledge a debt of gratitude to the two individuals who most influenced the writing of this book; my father, Philip Steinmetz, who introduced me to the treasures of Yiddish literature; and my teacher, Uriel Weinreich, who introduced me to the world of Yiddish scholarship.

✴ ✴ ✴ ✴

For this revised edition, I wish to thank all the readers who commented constructively on the book after its original publication, especially David L. Gold, editor of the *Jewish Language Review;* William Safire, language columnist for the *New York Times Magazine;* and Bella Hass Weinberg, consulting librarian of YIVO Institute for Jewish Research and editor of *Judaica Librarianship.* I am also grateful to Nicole Mitchell, director of The University of Alabama Press, acquisitions editor Judith Knight, assistant managing editor Suzette Griffith, and other members of the staff to whose efforts I owe publication of this new edition.

Yiddish
AND
English

Introduction

Over a hundred years have passed since the Yiddish language made its seminal contact with English on American soil. Brought about by historical accident, the crossing of these two languages proved to be unexpectedly fruitful, enriching both with many new speech forms. Word borrowing between Yiddish and English has been both sizable and reciprocal, perhaps to a greater degree than is customary between languages coming in direct contact through the immigration of one linguistic group into the country of another.

Borrowing of this type, which comes about through bilingual speakers (in this case Yiddish-English speakers) living side by side with monolinguals (English speakers), has been called "intimate borrowing," to distinguish it from the cultural borrowing that occurs when speakers of different languages make casual contact through reading, travel, commerce, and the like.[1]

According to the American linguist Leonard Bloomfield, "Cultural borrowing of speech-forms is ordinarily mutual; it is one-sided only to the extent that one nation has more to give than the other."[2] In contrast, "Intimate borrowing is one-sided: we distinguish between the *upper* or *dominant* language, spoken by the conquering or otherwise more privileged group, and the *lower* language, spoken by the subject people, or, as in the United States, by humble immigrants. The borrowing goes predominantly from the upper language to the lower, and it very often extends to speech-forms that are not connected with cultural novelties."[3]

This description of intimate borrowing generally fits the borrowing pattern of most immigrant languages in contact with English in the United States. English, the prestigious majority language, owes far less to such immigrant languages as German, Italian, Norwegian, and Polish than these languages, as transformed in this country, came to owe American English. Yet in the case of Yiddish, Bloomfield's generalization fails to do justice to the remarkable influence this "lower" language has exerted upon the "upper" language of this country. Unlike most other immigrant languages, Yiddish contributed to American English not only a host of religio-cultural terms but also an exceptional number of words and locutions that did not embody or represent cultural innovations. Thus, for example, no other immigrant language has provided English with such groups of words as the Yiddish-derived designations for various types of bunglers or fools: *shlemiel, shlemazl, shlump, shnuk, shmendrik, shmigege, shmo, nebish, klots, yold,* etc.[4] Clearly these words do not represent cultural novelties, inasmuch as English has plenty of equivalent words or at least fairly close approximations to these words; all one has to do is look into a good English thesaurus under the heading *fool.* English slang, however, is an area of the language that is in constant need of fresh *forms* to replace old forms that have become standard or obsolete, and Yiddish loans seem to fill this particular need eminently in slangy or informal American speech.[5]

The hunger of American English for new forms accounts in part for its borrowing of noncultural items from Yiddish. But the question remains, why Yiddish more than any other minority language? The answer may be found both in the nature of

Yiddish and in the history of its relationship to the English language in this country.

The purpose of the present work is to describe the history of this relationship and explore both its causes and its effects on the two languages. The broad canvas to be covered has dictated that the presentation be general and informal, more in the nature of a historical account than of a linguistic study.[6] Yet it is hoped that this effort will serve to stimulate interest in the subject of Yiddish-English contact and lead to further study of Jewish languages as well as of the broader fields of language contact and bilingualism.

The Appeal of Yiddish

1

In 1936, describing the influence of various immigrant languages on American English, H. L. Mencken wrote:

> In New York City the high density of Eastern Jews in the population has made almost every New Yorker familiar with a long list of Yiddish words, e.g. *kosher, shadchan, matzoth, mazuma, yom kippur, meshuggah, gefilte-fisch,* and many non-Jewish New Yorkers have added others that are not generally familiar, e.g. *schul, bar-mitzva, blintzes, kaddish, treyfa, dayyan, goy, dokus, shochet, schmus, shicker, schiksa, mohel, get, hesped, kishkes, kittl, meshummad,* and *pesach.* The Yiddish exclamation of *oi-yoi* is common New Yorkese, and Yiddish greetings, *mazzaltov* and *scholom aleichim,* are pretty well known and understood.[1]

Except for the reference to "Eastern Jews" (meaning Jewish immigrants from eastern Europe) and certain modifications in the spelling of Yiddish-origin words, the above passage might have been written today. For not only are the Yiddishisms listed by Mencken still widely used in English—albeit now, as then, mostly by English-speaking Jews—but they have been supplemented by many others which have attained remarkable currency among non-Jews across the United

States and, through American influence, in some other English-speaking countries of the world.

There is ample evidence, as we shall see later, that many of the Yiddishisms recorded by Mencken in the 1920s and 1930s had appeared in English as early as the 1880s, when the first large wave of East European Jews landed on these shores; indeed, Yiddish words crop up in American and British English writings of the early nineteenth century, many decades before the mass immigrations to this country and England began. But the real influx and dissemination of Yiddishisms in the United States did not occur until the immigrants and their children, eager to blend into the great American "melting pot," started to speak English in earnest, and in so doing, frequently injected into their speech many Yiddish words and expressions, along with Yiddish-influenced intonations, pronunciations, and grammatical constructions. Thus it was in the 1920s and 1930s, when Yiddish began to make inroads into the mainstream of American English, that students of Americana, such as Mencken, first took notice of Yiddish and other immigrant languages as a significant new development on the American cultural scene.

The influx of Yiddishisms into American English gained momentum during and following the period of World War II, when a revival of ethnic pride among American Jews sparked a renewed interest in Yiddish. Courses in Yiddish were introduced at various colleges and universities, impelling Uriel Weinreich to publish his important textbook, *College Yiddish,* in 1949. Interest in Yiddish continued unabated into the 1960s and reached an especially high point at the end of that decade. The popularity of Yiddish during the 1960s is attested by the almost simultaneous appearance of three widely read books on the subject: Leo Rosten's *The Joys of Yiddish* (1968), Lillian Mermin Feinsilver's *The Taste of Yiddish* (1970), and Maurice Samuel's *In Praise of Yiddish* (1971). Samuel was a distinguished author who had written many works on Jewish subjects, including books about Sholom Aleichem and I. L. Peretz; Feinsilver's well-documented studies of the influence of Yiddish on American English had appeared earlier in *American Speech* and many other journals; and Rosten, also a prolific writer on the subject and a noted humorist, popularized the portmanteau word Yinglish to designate Yiddish words that have become part of English.[2]

Nor did lexicographers fail to take note of the Yiddish phenomenon:

> In the past six years Yiddish borrowings (*chuzpa, klutz, megillah, shtick,* etc.) have entered the language in growing numbers.[3]

> The most current Yiddish slang terms in the 1960s included *nebbish* 'a sad sac,' *chutzpah* 'gall, nerve,' *yenta* 'a female busybody,' *klutz* 'a clumsy person,' *nosh* 'a snack' and in Great Britain 'food,' *mavin* 'an expert,' *mensch* 'a decent fellow,' *schlock* 'junk,' *kvell* 'delight,' *schlep* 'a jerk,' and *kvetch* 'a complainer.' Many of these terms function both as nouns and verbs (*to kvetch, to nosh*), and have also spawned derivatives, such as *klutzy* and *schlocky.*[4]

The attraction of Yiddish did not fade with the advent of the 1980s. Some measure of the continuity, if not growth, of interest in Yiddish was reflected in the highly popular *Jewish Catalog* series compiled by Sharon and Michael Strassfeld for the Jewish Publication Society of America. While *The First Jewish Catalog,* published in 1973, devoted six pages to a discussion of Yiddish, and *The Second Jewish Catalog* (1976) added another two pages of information, *The Third Jewish Catalog,* published in 1980, devoted to the subject of Yiddish no less than twenty-five pages. One of the best romanized lexicons of Yiddish, Samuel Rosenbaum's *A Yiddish Word Book for English-Speaking People,* appeared in 1978. This little book includes some two thousand Yiddish words transcribed in the romanization system of the YIVO Institute for Jewish Research, a corresponding English-Yiddish section, and a section of Yiddish proverbs and aphorisms. Capitalizing on the huge success of his earlier book, Leo Rosten published a sequel entitled *Hooray for Yiddish!* in 1982. Pale imitations of Rosten's popular books appeared regularly, among them an error-ridden book by Sidney J. Jacobs entitled *The Jewish Word Book: A Compendium of Popular Yiddish and Hebrew Words and Phrases That Color Our Vocabulary* (New York: Jonathan David Publishers, 1982)[5]; a shrilly humorous paperback entitled *Dictionary Shmictionary! A Yiddish and Yinglish Dictionary* (New York: Quill Publishers, 1983), by Paul Hoffman and Matt Freedman, whose saving grace is the use of numerous quotations using Yiddish-origin words; and a highly idiosyncratic collection of essays and essay-long definitions by the musician and folklorist Gene Bluestein, entitled *Anglish-Yinglish: Yiddish in American Life and Literature* (Athens, Georgia: University of Georgia Press, 1989).

There is no simple explanation for the long-lived Yiddish influence in American English. Writers on the subject have made much of the special ability of Yiddish words to express nuances—irony, wryness, deprecation, condescension, etc.—that are lacking in equivalent words in other languages. This is undoubtedly one of the attractions of Yiddish; it is well known that many languages have appropriated Yiddish words to add spice and color to colloquial speech. Among Dutch Jews, for example, Yiddish has disappeared as a language; yet Yiddish words absorbed by Dutch have not disappeared, and according to one writer such loanwords from Yiddish as *schofel* 'shabby,' *lef* 'heart,' *balleboos* 'householder,' *dalles* 'poverty,' *chappen* 'to steal,' *schiker* 'drunk,' and *sof* 'end' "have acquired Dutch citizenship and travel with Dutch passports."[6]

No doubt, also, the familiarity of people of different nationalities (Jews and non-Jews alike) with Yiddish words has

helped to keep the words alive in English. Over the centuries
Yiddish has attained the status of a world language, a kind of
lingua franca, among Jews of European Ashkenazic origin or
descent, enabling them to communicate with each other
whether they are Americans visiting Russia, Russians emigrat-
ing to Israel, or French Jews crossing the Channel into Britain.
Despite the lack of association of Yiddish with a native home-
land or a specific geographical base—there being no country
in which Yiddish is a national language—it has somewhat
paradoxically attained a longer life in all the countries to which
it was imported than many other transplanted immigrant languages, which tended quite naturally to be abandoned by the
immigrants in favor of the dominant languages of their adop-
tive countries.

Probably the most important factor in the preservation of the
contact between Yiddish and English is the attitude of modern
American Jews toward Yiddish. There was a time in Europe,
during the period preceding and following the turn of the century, when enlightened Jews looked upon this language as a
detestable low-class *zhargon* (jargon) and such a view was for
a time quite prevalent in this country too. Today, however,
most Jews regard Yiddish as an integral element of Jewish
culture. The continuing use of Yiddishisms among urban
American Jews is thus largely responsible for their cross-cul-
tural dissemination.[7]

This dissemination has been clearly abetted by certain factors of place and time which Feinsilver describes in *The Taste
of Yiddish* and elsewhere. These include (1) the common use
of Yiddishisms by the advertising and merchandising indus-
tries not only to appeal to the Jewish market and promote the
sale of Jewish foods and other products, but also to capitalize
on the novelty and humor of popular Yiddish words and expressions to attract consumers and stimulate sales; (2) the increased mobility of American Jews and Americans in general
that helps to circulate Yiddishisms (compare the relative im-

mobility of an ethnic group such as the Pennsylvania Germans, whose usages are sometimes curiously similar to Yiddish ones);[8] and (3) the growth in this century of the various communications media, especially in the field of entertainment, in which Jews have been prominently involved.

Taking all these factors into consideration, it is still remarkable that Yiddish has remained alive among American Jews for as long as it has considering, on the one hand, the relative smallness of the Jewish population in the United States and, on the other, the fact that the majority of American Jews no longer speak Yiddish.[9] One would have expected the culture (including language) of this small group to have become assimilated long ago into the pervasive mass culture of America, the way the cultures of other immigrant groups have tended to become engulfed or diluted in this country.

In order to appreciate the factors that prevented this from happening to Yiddish, it will be helpful to review briefly the history of the Yiddish language from its inception and then, in somewhat greater detail, the development of this language in the United States.

A Brief History of Yiddish

2

The history of the Yiddish language is closely bound up with the dispersion of the Jewish people during their long exile. In the course of the Diaspora the Jews customarily adopted the languages of the countries in which they settled; invariably, however, they modified these languages in various ways, chiefly by introducing into them elements from their ancestral Hebrew and Aramaic as well as from other languages they had assimilated in their migrations. These "Judaized" languages have come to be known as *Jewish languages*.[1] The long existence of Jewish languages attests to the fact that for most of their history Jews have been bilinguals.

Perhaps the earliest of the Jewish languages was a Hebrew-influenced form of Aramaic (known as Aramic or Targumic) spoken by the Jews of the Middle East after the Babylonian Exile in the sixth century B.C.E. Later Jewish languages, some of which developed extensive literatures, were Ebri ("Judeo-Persian"), Yahudic ("Judeo-Arabic"), and Yavanic ("Judeo-Greek"). Typically, Jewish languages served as everyday means of communication within the Jewish communities and were often used with only marginal awareness of the differences—in pronunciation, vocabulary, grammar—between them and the coterritorial languages on which they were based. Though Jewish languages were usually written in Hebrew characters (and read, as Hebrew, from right to left), they were considered by their users secular, temporary vernaculars, sharply distinguished from the ancient sacred Hebrew tongue which was the medium in which most religious and communal matters, scholarly exchanges, and literary activity were conducted.

Thus, with no special significance attached to them, Jewish languages tended to be easily replaced by other languages acquired through emigration or conquest. This pattern of adoption and replacement characterized the early Jewish languages, including several that were precursors of Yiddish in western Europe. But Yiddish itself, as the language which Ashkenazic Jews have clung to for a thousand years, is an exception to this pattern, as is Judezmo, the language of Jews of Spanish descent. The forces that made these Jewish languages endure despite the widespread migrations of its speakers are not well understood, and various theories have been proposed to account for them. A partial explanation is that in the evolution of a Jewish language a point may be reached where its users recognize it as something more than a casual medium of communication, as something that has become imbued with emotion, tradition, and perhaps even with a degree of sanctity by virtue of its Hebrew component and its long association with Jews and Judaism. When this point is reached, the language assumes the character and often the name of "mother tongue" (*mame loshn* in Yiddish) and can no longer be easily dislodged from its position of eminence by another language, though it may continue to retain the adaptive flexibility and receptiveness to borrowing that seems to be a characteristic of all Jewish languages.

Whatever the reasons may be for its longevity, Yiddish is a Jewish language that resisted for centuries the impact of various coterritorial languages to become eventually the mother tongue of an estimated eleven million Ashkenazic Jews before World War II.[2]

The development of Yiddish over the past thousand years is roughly divided into four periods: Earliest, Old, Middle, and Modern.[3] The Earliest Yiddish period arose about the ninth century, when Jews of northern France and northern Italy began to migrate into the German-speaking region of the Rhine Valley between the Moselle and Rhine rivers, in an area bounded by the cities of Cologne, Mainz, Worms, and Speyer which the Jews designated Loter (the kingdom of Lotharingia, modern Lorraine or Lothringen). Small Jewish communities had existed in the region for centuries before the arrival of the newcomers; there is, for example, a Jewish tombstone in Cologne dating from the fourth century. But all that is known about the language of the Jews of the region before the 1100s is that it was *leshon 'ashkenaz,* the language of Germany.[4]

The new immigrants, many of them refugees from persecutions in France and Italy, brought with them a Jewish language they called Loez, which consisted of several Romance dialects containing varying admixtures of Hebrew and Aramaic words.[5] The influence of the Loez-speaking immigrants must have been considerable, for some of the oldest and commonest Yiddish words and names are of Loez origin: for example, *bentshn* 'to say the blessing after a meal,' from Latin *benedicere* 'to bless' through Old Italian, and *leyenen* 'to read (the Torah),' from Latin *legere* 'to read' through Gallo-Romance, both with the Germanic verb suffix *-n, -en; tsholnt* 'a Sabbath dish of slowly simmering meat and vegetables,' through Old French from Latin *calentem* 'warming, being warm'; the male name *Bunim,* from Old French *Bonhomme,* literally, 'good man,' and the female name *Yentl,* from Old Italian *Gentile,* literally, 'noble, genteel.'[6] According to Max Weinreich, the Yiddish word *shul* 'synagogue,' which is usually derived from Middle High German *schuol(e)* 'school' (itself a loanword from Latin *schola*), is actually a Loez word whose initial *sk-* sound was altered by influence of the German word to *sh-*.[7]

The Jewish immigrants arriving in Loter spoke two varieties

of Loez: Western Loez, the Jewish correlate of Old French, and Southern Loez, the Jewish correlate of Old Italian. The Jews of Loter, in turn, spoke a particular blend of medieval High German city dialects. What the two groups had in common linguistically was the ancient Hebrew-Aramaic substratum they shared. This fact is essential to an understanding of the reason why Yiddish came into being.

Hebrew-Aramaic was already integrated into the languages of the Jews. Now, with the confluence of the two varieties of Loez and the Jewish German of Loter, the Hebrew-Aramaic stratum of both sets of speakers was reinforced. The fusion of these three elements, German, Hebrew-Aramaic, and Romance —a fusion clearly represented by words like *bentshn* and *leyenen*—marked the emergence of Old Yiddish (1250–1500).

Although many Old Yiddish words appear to be identical with words recorded in various dialects of Middle High German, there is evidence that the Old Yiddish pronunciation of certain words had already diverged from that of the German. To some extent this is a matter of interpretation, since the Yiddish texts of that period, including the oldest (such as the Worms *makhzer* or holiday prayer book of 1272, and the Cambridge Codex of 1382) are written in Hebrew characters, as indeed most Jewish languages were and Yiddish and Judezmo still are. But there can be little doubt that the extent of divergence of Old Yiddish from the High German vocabulary and grammar of that time was substantial. Not only did Old Yiddish contain the Loez and Hebrew-Aramaic lexical components, but at the time of its earliest attestation in writing it contained German words that were already archaic or obsolete in the German dialects of the time.

It was during the Old Yiddish period that Jews began to move from Germany eastward as the Crusades swept across western Europe bringing with them Jewish persecution and the Black Death (1348–49). The migration of Yiddish speakers to Slavic countries turned out to be a crucial development in the history of Yiddish, for it not only removed Yiddish from the sphere of German influence but placed it under the influence of such Slavic languages as Polish, Ukrainian, and Belorussian.

During the Middle Yiddish period (1500–1700), the language came into its own as it flourished in Slavic soil. As a result of the increasing isolation of the original German-Jewish communities, coupled with continuous expulsions from German and Austrian cities that drove masses of Jews into Poland and further east, Yiddish broke away from the German dialects and developed dialects of its own. These dialects became more and more pronounced as Jews settled in increasingly large numbers in eastern Europe. Here the contact with Slavic languages introduced a host of new words and expressions into the language: verbs like *praven* 'to observe, celebrate,' *hodeven* 'bring up, raise,' *mutshen* 'harass, nag'; nouns like *pushke* 'box,' *kantshik* 'whip,' *blote* 'mud,' *shmate* 'rag'; adverbs like *take* 'indeed,' *khotsh(e)* 'at least, although'; adjectives like *paskudne* 'nasty'; interjections like *nu* 'well, so,' *zhe* 'then, so'; and a number of suffixes such as *-nyu, -ke, -tshe, -ets,* and *-nik.* The Slavic influence also affected the syntax, stress pattern, and semantics of Yiddish.

The dialectal development of Yiddish in eastern Europe resulted in a major divergence between Western Yiddish, spoken in Germany, Holland, Switzerland, and Alsace-Lorraine, and Eastern Yiddish, which is roughly classified into three major dialects: Southeastern (Ukrainia, Rumania, and eastern Galicia), Central (Poland and western Galicia), and Northeastern (Lithuania, Latvia, and Belorussia). With the advent of the Modern Yiddish period in 1700, Western Yiddish ceased to develop further and began a slow process of decline that by this century seemed nearly complete.

Eastern Yiddish, in great contrast, continued to thrive. In the latter half of the eighteenth century the growing movement of Hasidism transformed Eastern Yiddish into a vehicle of fervent pietistic expression, enriching and formalizing it as the language of the religious masses. A synchronous though diametrically opposite development, the rise of the Haskalah or Jewish Enlightenment, gave Yiddish a secular direction by using it as a medium for disseminating its ideas among the Yiddish-speaking masses. Though Yiddish Haskalah literature was narrow in scope, being primarily devoted to anti-Hasidic and didactic works, its effective use of Yiddish became the basis for the development of modern standard literary Yiddish, a language notable for the unique fusion of what Uriel Weinreich described as "its multiple origins: German, Hebrew-Aramaic, Romance, Slavic, and 'international' (modern technical and scientific vocabulary)."[8] It remained for the great Yiddish writer Sholem-Yankev Abramovitsh (1836–1917), creator of the immortal Mendele Moykher-Sforim, "Mendele, the bookseller," to overcome the limitations of earlier Hasidic and Haskalah literature and forge out of various literary and dialectal forms a modern, uniform Yiddish language that influenced the classic works of I. L. Peretz (1852–1915), Sholom Aleichem (1859–1916), Yehoash (1872–1927), Abraham Reisen (1876–1953), Sholem Asch (1880–1957), and other giants of modern Yiddish literature.

Thus, by the end of the nineteenth century Yiddish had become the universally recognized language of Ashkenazic Jews. It was this language that was brought to America from eastern Europe in the 1880s.

Yiddish in the United States

3

In the latter part of the nineteenth century, the growth of anti-Semitism in eastern Europe sparked a large-scale movement of Jewish emigration to the United States. As conditions steadily worsened in the 1870s, culminating in the Russian pogroms of 1881 and the infamous May Laws of 1882 (designed as "temporary edicts" but not abolished until February 1917), the migratory wave soon turned into an irresistible flood. Between 1877 and 1917 about two and a half million Jews reached the shores of this country, swamping the earlier Jewish population, which in 1870 amounted to a mere 250,000.[1] The language these immigrants brought with them was Yiddish.

Though the Yiddish of the immigrants consisted of several dialects and many local and regional varieties, it was an easier means of communication than such different and often mutually unintelligible languages as Russian, Rumanian, Polish, or English. And more importantly, Yiddish was the *mame loshn*, the mother tongue that united these millions of people and gave them a sense of identity. Not only was it their common language, but Yiddish was the core around which a great body of literature, folklore, and history had been built.

Thus, from the 1880s onward, the United States became a fertile soil for the transplanted Yiddish language and culture as the masses of poor Jews, huddled in the tenements of New

York's Lower East Side, Chicago's West Side, Boston's North End, and the ghettos of other large cities, strove to adapt their *shtetl* culture and their *yidishkayt* (traditional Judaism, Jewish way of life) to the demands and realities of urban American life.

This proved to be a hard task for the newcomers. True, they had obtained freedom from persecution, but at a price they had never dreamed of. Despised and ignored by the established "native" Jews, who considered them dirty, lazy, shiftless, and a nuisance to themselves, "a bane to the country and a curse to the Jews,"[2] having to work endless hours in unsanitary sweatshops for pitiful wages, living in cramped quarters often with as many as eight in a room, the immigrants were sorely tempted to give up the old ways and become Americanized as soon as possible. Many chose that road, but the vast majority, perhaps unable to break through the ghetto walls, retained their link with the past. The religious Jews organized synagogues, Hebrew schools, ritual baths, kosher stores, and charitable institutions, in all of which the language spoken was Yiddish. Jews who had become radicalized in Europe found in the free political atmosphere of America the opportunity to organize other types of institutions, political, educational, social, and cultural, such as trade unions and *landsmanshaftn,* societies whose members came from the same home towns in Europe. These Jews, too, used Yiddish at their meetings, in their publications, and at their rallies. Yiddish, in effect, was the principal language of American Jews at home and in the streets from the late 1880s to the late 1920s.

During this period Yiddish cultural activity, flourishing in the freedom denied it in eastern Europe, found intense expression in poetry, fiction, drama, journalism, and scholarship. A conference of Yiddish writers held in New York City about 1904 adopted a resolution that Yiddish be regarded as the national language of the Jews. It is noteworthy that this conference preceded by four years the famous Czernowitz Yiddish language conference (August 30–September 4, 1908) at which Yiddish was proclaimed a national language (not *the* national language, for that would have conflicted with Hebrew), thereby endowing Yiddish with prestige and laying the foundation for the flowering of Yiddish literature and scholarship in the twentieth century.

One of the major achievements of the Yiddish press in America at the turn of the century was the gradual elimination of *daytshmerish*—the pseudo-German style of Yiddish writing and speech which had dominated much of "enlightened" fiction and drama of the late nineteenth century. *Daytshmerish* at its worst not only replaced many Yiddish words with German ones but added to the mélange many unnecessary Anglicisms. Two newspapers, the *Arbeter tsaytung* and the *Fraye arbeter shtime*, both founded in 1890, were the first to drive the Germanized Yiddish out of their pages. Others soon followed suit.

In New York City, the center of the Yiddish-speaking population, over 150 different Yiddish newspapers, magazines, and other periodicals made their appearance between 1885 and 1914. The first Yiddish daily newspaper in America was the *Yidishes tageblat,* founded by Kasriel Hersch Sarasohn in 1885, less than ten years after the first Yiddish daily in the world, *Der yidisher telegraf,* appeared in Bucharest, Rumania. The most influential of all American Yiddish periodicals was the militantly socialist *Forverts* or *Jewish Daily Forward,* founded in 1897, which under the editorship of Abraham Cahan broadened its ideological base and attained a huge circulation, becoming an extremely popular family paper filled with news, stories, essays, poetry, book reviews, letters, humor, history lessons, and lessons in English.

Yiddish publications provided Yiddish poets and writers with the opportunity to reach large audiences, and groups of poets, such as *Di yunge* ("The Young") in the teens of the century and the *Inzikhistn* ("Introspectivists") a decade later, became famous both for the beauty of their work and the particularly modern American view of life they held out. The Yiddish newspapers and magazines were as a rule openly in favor of assimilation to the American way of life, and had no scruples about freely admitting into Yiddish all types of Anglicisms. The younger Yiddish writers and poets, on the other hand, while as secular and Americanophile in orientation as the periodicals, tried to keep the language free of American English influences. There were at the same time strong Orthodox elements in the Jewish population that opposed assimilation in any form, and it was largely in reaction to the growing secular influence of the *Forverts* that in 1901 Jacob Saphirstein established the *Morgn zhurnal* or *Jewish Morning Journal*, which represented the Orthodox point of view.

The Jewish theater was also thriving, not only on New York's Second Avenue, but also in Chicago, Philadelphia, Boston, Detroit, and Cleveland. The first Yiddish play in the United States was performed in 1882. Initially the plays were unashamedly sentimental and melodramatic. But in the early 1890s Jacob Adler and Jacob Gordin introduced serious drama on the Yiddish stage, beginning a golden era of the Yiddish theater that lasted into the late 1920s. The Yiddish secular school system also reached a peak during the 1920s, with an enrollment of about twelve thousand children.

But even as the feverish cultural activity centering on Yiddish was at its height, the process of acculturation of the immigrants and their children to the American environment was moving apace, foreshadowing the decline of Yiddish. Ironically, it was the Yiddish press and the Yiddish arts which most glorified the American experience and encouraged acculturation, thereby accelerating their own decline in this country. Abraham Cahan's insistence on the need to learn English eventually led to the demise of the great daily which he helped establish. The fact that the two tendencies—preservation of Yiddish culture and hastening of the Americanizing process—ran counter to each other was not as yet fully realized at that time.

For a period of about forty years Yiddish remained the dominant language of American Jewry, reaching its zenith in the late 1920s, when it began to be eclipsed by English. This was the fate which to a greater or lesser degree overtook most of the immigrant languages in this country. In his series of broadcasts entitled *America,* Alistair Cooke vividly described the process of Americanization:

> The quicker a boy or girl learnt to speak American English, the sooner his schoolmates would stop calling him a Kraut or a Polack or a Wop—which was fine for the children but tough on the parents. The children went home and they saw their parents reading an Italian or a Yiddish newspaper and they began to notice the thick accents and they felt uncomfortable, and they felt ashamed. This is a great and tragic theme in American life and literature, and inevitably there came, and comes, the time when the parents, too, go to school, to learn the language of their sons and daughters.[3]

Though the Americanizing process was largely internal, after World War I it assumed the rather sinister guise of an open movement and even of public policy, with the immigrant languages as its main target. In the words of one writer on the subject of linguistic chauvinism:

> Americanization placed a special emphasis on extirpating the languages of the immigrants, for the obvious reason that language carries the culture of its speakers. Get rid of the language—and the nation has also rid itself of the alien's instrument of perception, his means of expressing foreign values, his maintenance of a culture transported from another continent. Theodore Roosevelt's statement in 1919 is typical of the Americanization position:

> We have room for but one language here and that is the English language, for we intend to see that the crucible turns our people out as Americans and not as dwellers in a polyglot boarding house.
>
> The Americanization movement reached its height in the 1930s, but its effects continue to be felt. Every census since then has revealed that fewer Americans claim a non-English mother tongue.[4]

The devastating effect of Americanization on Yiddish, as on the other immigrant languages, cannot be minimized. But other factors also contributed to the decline of these languages. A major contributor was the Johnson Act of 1924, which drastically reduced immigration by a quota system, thus stemming the influx of immigrants who had kept infusing new blood into the Yiddish-speaking community. Another blow was the Crash of 1929 and subsequent Great Depression, which ruined financially many Yiddish cultural institutions, notably the Yiddish theater.

By the 1930s it was a commonplace to say that the days of Yiddish were counted. Though millions of Jews still spoke or understood Yiddish, their morale had sunk to a very low ebb, as indeed the entire country's morale had fallen with the Depression. Yet even during those dark days of widespread poverty and rampant anti-Semitism (in 1933 there were over one hundred fascist organizations in the United States, many with direct ties to the Nazis), when Jews tried to pass as Gentiles and a Yiddish accent was a butt of jokes and a brand of shame, even then Yiddish was still widely spoken and written in this country. According to Fishman, "Yiddish radio programs seem to have enjoyed their greatest following from the mid-thirties through to the conclusion of the Second World War."[5] The Yiddish press in the 1930s was far from dead; in 1930 there were eleven Yiddish dailies and in 1940 there were ten.

Yiddish continued to be used in the Yiddish secular schools maintained by the Workman's Circle (*Arbeter Ring*) and the Jewish National Workers Alliance (*Farband*), as well as in many of the Orthodox religious schools. One heard Yiddish in the synagogues, in Jewish cultural and charitable organizations, in the Catskill mountains of New York where Jews spent the summer living in *kokhaleyns* (bungalows with cooking facilities, lit., 'cook alones')—one heard Yiddish almost every place where Jews gathered. English had become their primary language, but Yiddish remained a handy and folksy second language.

The use of Yiddish among the masses of American Jews continued to decline through the 1940s and the following decades down to the end of the century. There is no denying that the decline persists; but there is equally no denying that Yiddish has shown an amazing viability for a language whose imminent death has been predicted time and again for the past hundred years. Such prophecies actually precede the American experience. In 1862 Alexander Zederbaum, the pioneer of Hebrew journalism in Russia, told Czarist authorities that Yiddish was a dying language. And in 1899 a distinguished historian of Yiddish language and literature, Leo Wiener, concluded his book, *The History of Yiddish Literature in the Nineteenth Century,* with the observation that Yiddish in America "is certainly doomed to extinction. Its lease on life is commensurate with the large immigration to the New World. In the countries of Europe, it will last as long as [Jews] are secluded in ghettos and driven into pales."[6]

Prophcies of doom notwithstanding, Yiddish continues to survive in America. To say that it is thriving, as some enthusiasts of the language are wont to, is to indulge in wishful thinking. But to say that it is dead or dying is just as unrealistic. In the first place, no language with a great literature can be considered dead: Hebrew was not spoken by most Jews for two thousand years, yet it was hardly dead as long as the Torah and the Jewish prayers were studied and read; Latin is not dead as long as Cicero and Virgil are taught and read in the original. There are such things as extinct languages, but as long as Yiddish literature—its poetic, dramatic, and literary masterpieces—will be read and studied, it will never become extinct.

Secondly, a language with nearly four million speakers worldwide (see Chapter 2, note 2) can scarcely be in the throes of death. In the mid-1980s, there were more than seventy-five Yiddish periodicals, including seven dailies, published in Buenos Aires, New York, Paris, and Tel Aviv; there are also thirty-five Yiddish theatrical companies in these and various other large cities.[7] In Israel, where English was once denigrated as a *galut* (Diaspora) tongue, it is now generally accepted.[8] In Sweden, Jewish emigrants from Poland have been publishing since 1976 a Yiddish magazine entitled *Yidishe kultur in Skandinavie,* and a similar periodical called *Afsnay* ("Anew") is published in Denmark. *Undzer shtime* ("Our Voice"), a magazine published in Paris, reported that in October 1981 a group of French students formed an organization to study and spread Yiddish culture. And in the former Soviet Union, the only Yiddish magazine, *Sovetish heymland,* brought out in 1980 a small supplement (sixty-four pages) of Yiddish lessons for beginners, the first such textbook published in the Soviet Union since before World War II. (The official Institute of Jewish Affairs also announced the publication in 1984 of a new forty-thousand-word Russian-Yiddish dictionary, which had been originally scheduled to appear in 1948.) So any prognosis about the fate of Yiddish in the United States is not ipso facto applicable to the fate of Yiddish in Great Britain, Latin America, Canada, South Africa, Russia, or elsewhere.

But what about Yiddish in the United States? Its survival up to the present has been attributed to a number of factors which can be summarized as follows:

(1) Continuous immigration of Yiddish speakers. Even as

American-born Jews stopped using Yiddish as their primary language, the ranks of the Jewish population were periodically supplemented by new arrivals who spoke Yiddish and kept renewing the use of the language.[9] This happened during the World War II period and after the Hungarian Revolution of 1956, and it is happening at the present time, with new contingents of Yiddish-speaking immigrants from the Soviet Union arriving yearly to this country.

(2) Resurgence of Jewish ethnicity since the 1940s. If, as has been contended by some Jewish historians, American Jews stood on the verge of assimilation in the 1930s, they were rescued from this peril by the rise of nazism and fascism in Europe, which rekindled their sense of identification with their ancient culture. Undoubtedly loyalty to the Jewish past was revived by the tragedy of the Holocaust and greatly reinforced by the establishment of Israel as a Jewish state. These events not only caused a resurgence of interest in the Yiddish language but enhanced with prestige this once despised "immigrant" language.

(3) Return of the third generation. Along with other ethnic groups, the American Jewish community has seen a remarkable renewal of interest in its roots among the Jews who constitute the third-generation descendants of the original immigrants. The members of the second generation, the children of the immigrants,

> seeking to find a place in American society, often gave up their Jewish identity or drifted away from it. At the time, Americans believed in the "melting pot" theory, when all newcomers were expected to dissolve their cultural identities. However, the children of the second generation have, in astonishing numbers, rejected the doctrine of the "melting pot" and have taken their Jewish cultural identity with utmost seriousness. They identify with Jews everywhere, and they are deeply involved in exploring their Jewish past as well as the living elements of contemporary Jewish culture.[10]

The rediscovery of Yiddish by members of the third generation has been largely responsible for the introduction of Yiddish studies in many colleges and universities in the United States. (4) Loyality to Yiddish. The dedication of many American Jews to Yiddish has been only equaled by the millenia-old devotion of Jews to their sacred language, Hebrew. The ranks of devoted Yiddishists in this country include some religious but mostly nonreligious Jews. It is the latter group that over the lean years continued to run Yiddish culture schools and encouraged work in Yiddish literature and scholarship. There are still a number of Workmen's Circle culture *shules* (schools) operating successfully in various cities of the United States and Canada.[11] But among the religious groups, it is principally the so-called ultra-Orthodox and Hasidic Jews that continue to use Yiddish as a primary language in their homes and schools. Contrasting Yiddish with other Jewish languages of the past and present, Uriel Weinreich wrote: "The language loyalty of the Yiddish-speaking community has not been equaled among the speakers of Dzhudezmo ("Judeo-Spanish") or other Jewish Languages."[12]

As of this writing, the renewed interest in Yiddish among many American Jews of varying ages and ideologies has not yet waned. There have been, however, a few serious setbacks to devout Yiddishists in recent years. The greatest blow has been the rapid decline of the old Yiddish dailies, which have been plagued by circulation problems since the 1940s. First the *Jewish Day-Morning Journal (Der tog-Morgn zhurnal)*, which was born in 1953 when *Der tog* (established in 1914) absorbed the *Morgn zhurnal,* ceased publication on December 28, 1971. Then, perhaps more traumatically, the long-lived daily *Forverts* was converted to a weekly in 1982. Unfortunately, these dramatic reverses have tended to obscure the positive aspects of the current Yiddish scene.

In the 1980s, over twenty Yiddish periodicals, chiefly weeklies and monthlies, were published in the United States, including such long-established ones as *Di tsukunft* (1892), the *Forverts* (1897), the weekly *Yidisher kemfer* (1906), the leftist *Morgn frayhayt* (1922), and such comparative newcomers as the Orthodox weeklies *Der yid* (1954) and the *Algemeyner zhurnal* (1972). Among the most important literary periodicals were *Di Goldene keyt* ("The Golden Chain"), a quarterly edited in Israel by Avrom Sutskever; *Yidishe Kultur,* edited by I. Goldberg; *Afn shvel* ("On the Threshold"), an influential quarterly, organ of the New York–based League for Yiddish, Inc., edited by Mordkhe Schaechter; *Yugntruf* ("The Call of Youth"), a quarterly of the Yiddish youth movement, edited by young adults since 1964; *Kinder Zhurnal* ("Children's Journal"), a quarterly edited by Bella Gottesman; *Yidishe shprakh* ("The Yiddish Language"), edited by Mordkhe Schaechter; and, since 1994, the scholarly journal *Khulyot* ("Links"), dedicated to Yiddish literary research and published in Israel by the Faculties of Humanities of the Universities of Haifa and Tel-Aviv, with Shalom Luria and Haya bar-Yitzchak as editors.

There is, in Fishman's words, "a tremendous urge to live, a veritable élan-vital in the world of Yiddish."[13] This passionate urge to keep Yiddish alive, whether driven by nostalgia, the search for roots, or by a need to reaffirm Jewish cultural identity in the post-Holocaust era, was strikingly manifested in the 1990s, when Yiddish study and research suddenly emerged from relative obscurity into the wide-open world of cyberspace. On May 15, 1991, Yiddish made its online debut with the introduction of *Mendele,*[14] a forum dedicated to the exchange of news and information about Yiddish language and literature. Initially circulating among a handful of academics, by the year 2000 Mendele numbered 2,300 subscribers located in twenty-four countries and in every continent except Antarctica. In April, 1997, Mendele launched *The Mendele Review,* a literary supplement edited by Leonard Prager of the University of Haifa. Subscription to Mendele is free. The e-mail address for postings is <mendele@lists.yale.edu>.

On the World Wide Web, Mendele is accessed at <http://www2.trincoll.edu/~mendele>.

On its Web site, Mendele offers a cornucopia of information, including a gallery of Yiddish writers, ways of improving one's Yiddish, stories, novels, poems, and other texts in Yiddish (some also rendered in romanized form), as well as links to various Yiddish Web pages and periodicals, such as the *Forverts, Der Yidisher TamTam, Der Bavebter Yid, and Yugntruf*. It also provides a list of more than sixty other Yiddish-related sites on the World Wide Web, among them "The Yiddish Voice," a weekly Yiddish radio show; "Zemerl," an interactive database of more than 400 Jewish songs, half of which are in Yiddish; the Web site of the National Yiddish Book Center in Amherst, Mass. <www.yiddishbooks.com>, which holds a collection of 1.4 million out-of-print Yiddish books; "Virtual Shtetl," a Yiddish language and culture site; a klezmer music Web page, maintained by Ari Davidow; "UYIP" (Understanding Yiddish Information Processing), a forum on using computers in Yiddish; the "Spoken Yiddish Language Project," which presents digitized samples of spoken Yiddish; the Arbeter Ring (Workmen's Circle) Web site; the Yamada Web Guide to Yiddish; and a Web site listing yearly international programs, institutes, and events involving Yiddish language and culture, of which there were thirty major ones in the year 2000 in the United States, Canada, England, Germany, France, Belgium, Russia, Lithuania, and Ukraine.

A word about Yiddish scholarship. The hub around which Yiddish cultural and linguistic research revolves in the United States, and from which it radiates to the world of Yiddish beyond America, is the YIVO Institute for Jewish Research. YIVO is an acronym for *Yidisher Visnshaftlikher Institut,* or Jewish Scientific Institute, which was the organization's original English name. YIVO was founded in 1925 in Berlin, but Vilna (Vilnius) was chosen as its center, with branches in Berlin, Warsaw, and New York. When in 1940 the Soviet authorities closed down Jewish cultural institutions in Lithuania (followed by the Nazi occupation of Vilna in 1941), the American branch of YIVO became the organization's headquarters. Since then, YIVO has grown in size and in activities. It awards yearly fellowships to Yiddish scholars and holds conferences, seminars, and exhibits all year round. It publishes and sponsors many works in fields as diverse as linguistics, folklore, psychology, sociology, literature, history, and economics. It lists among its publications *YIVO Bleter* (founded in 1931), dealing with Jewish scholarly research; *Yidishe shprakh* (founded in 1941); *Yedies fun YIVO* ("News of the YIVO"), a bilingual newsletter; the *YIVO Annual of Jewish Social Science,* an English-language biennial launched in 1946; and the multi-volume *Language and Culture Atlas of Ashkenazic Jewry* (edited by Marvin Herzog, 1992–1999). The organization's building in New York City houses a vast library of Judaica and over two million items in its archives. The YIVO Web site is found at <http://www.yivoinstitute.org>.

To sum up this brief discussion of the fortunes of Yiddish in this country, we might say that the language has undergone three stages in its 100-odd years of existence in the United States: it flourished during the "golden age" of Yiddish, from the last two decades of the nineteenth century through the 1920s; it declined as the primary language of American Jews in the 1930s and 1940s; and finally, it continued to be used as either a second or as a primary language down to the present, with a slow but continuous decline in the number of its speakers but with a marked renewal of interest in its preservation since the post-World War II period.

According to the United States Census Bureau's National Population Estimates for 1990, a total of 213,064 individuals five years or older gave Yiddish as the language spoken at home. These included 151,377 Yiddish-English bilinguals who speak English very well, 44,213 who speak English well, and 15,431 who do not speak English well. (At this writing, the

U.S. Census Bureau's figures for the year 2000 have not yet been published.) The figure of 213,064 in 1990 shows a comparatively small drop from that of 234,000 Yiddish speakers listed a decade earlier in the Census of 1980. Both figures, however, are a far cry from the skewed estimate of 1,500,000 supplied by the 1970 Census, which required subjects to give their "mother tongue" (defined as the language spoken at home when the person was a child, not necessarily the language now spoken or used). A more realistic estimate was the figure of 964,000 Yiddish speakers provided by the 1960 Census. But this leads to the startling conclusion that in the thirty years between 1960 and 1990 a huge chunk of over 700,000 American Jews stopped using Yiddish. This may be true. But contrary to the popular wisdom, statistical figures have been known to lie, and it is risky to draw conclusive inferences from them. (Note, for example, that in the Census of 1930, only 1,222,658 Jews gave Yiddish as their mother tongue!)[15]

Even if we take the statistics at their face value, however, the prospects of the continuity of Yiddish in the United States are brighter today than they were just ten years ago thanks to the new resources for study and scholarship provided by the Internet. And it is hard to ignore the status of Yiddish among the non-English languages spoken in the United States. The 1990 Census ranks Yiddish as the sixteenth among the fifty non-English languages, just behind Russian, but well ahead of languages like Hungarian (twenty-second), Hebrew (twenty-third), Dutch (twenty-fourth), and Serbocroatian (thirty-fourth).[16] Moreover, demographers have projected that among those who in the Census of 2000 will give Yiddish as their first or second language, there will be 26,000 children from ultra-Orthodox homes whose primary and perhaps *only* language will be Yiddish, a gain of twenty percent over the projected number for 1985.[17]

All this should be gratifying news to Yiddish speakers who, having listened to doomsayers for years, have grown despondent over the fate of their language.

The Americanization of Yiddish

4

In the very first issue, January–February 1941, of *Yidishe shprakh,* a Yiddish scholarly journal published in New York and devoted to the Yiddish language, the line of battle was drawn between the "purists" and the "permissivists," between those who would guard the mother tongue from being polluted by unhealthy foreign influences (in this case, from American English) and those who saw nothing "pure" about language in the first place and willingly extended a warm welcome to any new borrowing. This is a familiar theme to many speakers of modern European languages, such as the French (witness the furor over Franglais, the wholesale import of Americanisms into French), the Germans, and the Russians, though not to modern English speakers, whose receptiveness to borrowings is well known. Yet, curiously, it is a theme that runs through the history of Yiddish in this country.

The liberal position toward borrowing from American English was stated by the noted Yiddish writer and critic Shmuel Niger: "Such words as *pedler, blof, beybi, olraytnik* were included by Alexander Harkavy in his dictionary. So let us say: It is permissible! These are legitimate Yiddish words."[1]

The opposing position was taken in the same issue of *Yidishe shprakh* by the eminent Yiddish linguist, Max Weinreich, who, though by no means a purist, felt that the line must be drawn somewhere.[2] Weinreich argued cogently that it was not the changed concepts (such as that *strit* implies more than the corresponding Yiddish *gas,* both meaning 'street') that brought about Americanization of Yiddish, but the social prestige of English. The Yiddish speaker wanted to talk English but could not; but using English words such as *desk* instead of *shraybtish, shur* 'sure' instead of *zikher,* and *strit* instead of *gas,* helped him feel more up to date, more Americanized. It was necessary, therefore, to distinguish between two different types of borrowings from English: those that represented new and specifically American concepts, such as *yunyen* 'union,' *beysbol* 'baseball,' *dzhez* 'jazz,' and *blof* 'bluff,' and those that needlessly replaced legitimate Yiddish words of identical meaning, such as *boy* (replacing *yingl*), *strit* (replacing *gas*), and *vinde* 'window,' replacing *fentster.*

By 1941, when this debate took place, Yiddish in this country had over a period of sixty years absorbed perhaps thousands of loanwords from American English, thanks in large measure to the Americanizing efforts of newspapers like the *Forverts,* which encouraged the use of "potato Yiddish," a Yiddish-English mixture patterned on the speech of uneducated immigrant Jews.

But, as Weinreich suggested, the immigrant Jew knew no better and could hardly be blamed. Given the hostile conditions under which Yiddish labored in this country, as the language of poor and lowly immigrants eager to become as American as possible, it was inevitable that the Yiddish of the newcomers should become quickly Americanized, absorbing from English not only a large vocabulary and numerous idioms but also diverse morphological and syntactic elements.

Judah A. Joffe described the development of American Yiddish as follows:

> Conveniently, though not strictly, it may be said that American Yiddish began to develop with mass immigration after the

Russian pogroms of 1881 to 1882. The newcomers were thrown into the rushing American life with its wealth of unfamiliar objects, surroundings, conditions and ideas for which they had no ready terms. Their adjustment to these novel scenes necessitated the adoption of new designations: furthermore, the "path of least resistance" and the desire not to be dubbed "greenhorns" caused English words to elbow out deeply-rooted Yiddish terms in many instances. The new element in Yiddish was treated on an equal footing with the other traditional components (Middle High German, Hebrew, and Slavic) in the course of their adaptation to the New World.[3]

The most obvious feature of American Yiddish is the extent of its lexical borrowing from English.[4] Countless nouns, verbs, adjectives, and adverbs of the English common vocabulary have been appropriated and integrated into the Yiddish phonological and morphological system. A typical sentence by a Yiddish speaker might be: *Der loyer in mayn bilding geyt mufn tsum beysment flor* 'The lawyer in my building is going to move to the basement floor,' which contains no less than five English loanwords: *loyer, bilding, mufn, beysment,* and *flor.*

Many of the English loanwords are of the sort Max Weinreich approved, natural adoptions into Yiddish because equivalent Yiddish terms are lacking. For example: *sobvey* 'subway,' *kemp* 'summer camp,' *eleveyter* 'elevator,' *intervyu* 'interview,' *gengster* 'gangster,' *londre* 'laundry,' *nikl* 'nickel,' *muvis* 'movies,' *hayskul* 'high school,' *ayzkrim* 'ice cream,' etc.[5]

The largest group of loanwords, however, are those that have Yiddish equivalents, but that by force of everyday usage simply replace or supersede the Yiddish words. Core-vocabulary terms such as *bikoz* 'because,' *enivay* 'anyway,' *okey* 'OK,' *bize* 'busy,' *kar* 'car,' *regele* 'regular,' *stor* 'store,' *biznes* 'business,' *kitshn* 'kitchen,' *brekfes* 'breakfast,' *koner* 'corner,' *beybi* 'baby,' *brentsh* 'branch,' *trobl* 'trouble,' *saper* 'supper,' *tsher* 'chair,' *leter* 'letter,' *piktshe* 'picture,' *padi* 'party,' and hundreds of others fall into this category. Most of these words are not recognized as part of standard Yiddish, though they are widely used in colloquial American Yiddish. Even such idiomatic and conventional expressions as *afkoz* 'of course,' *gudbay* 'good-bye,' *nevermayn* 'never mind,' *olrayt* 'all right,' *pliz* 'please,' *shur* 'sure,' and various forms of address, e.g., *mister, kozn* 'cousin,' have become parts of everyday speech, though not accepted in formal or literary American Yiddish.

A separate large class of English words that have become part of standard Yiddish (i.e., the modern literary language) are words of an international character. Most of these words are polysyllabic and usually come from the intellectual sphere. This class includes such words as *konventsionel* 'conventional,' *prezentabl* 'presentable,' *panorame* 'panorama,' *laboratoriye* 'laboratory,' *eksistentsiyelizm* 'existentialism.' New terms from science and technology belong in this group: *astronoyt* 'astronaut,' *propeler, plastik, telekontrol, satelit* 'satellite,' etc.

The continuous and often indiscriminate borrowing from American English is confirmed by an examination of almost any of the various Yiddish periodicals, especially newspapers, published in this country. An example is the December 1, 1975 issue of the *Forverts*. Scanning the first five pages of this issue I found a considerable number of English borrowings which are not recorded in Uriel Weinreich's *Modern English-Yiddish Yiddish-English Dictionary,* a standard reference work that includes most English words that have become naturalized or that Weinreich found acceptable in American Yiddish.[6] The following is a list of the unrecorded American English borrowings: *front-liniye* 'front line,' *sekreteri ov steyt* 'secretary of state,' *steytment* 'statement,' *krismes* 'Christmas,' *menefektsherer* 'manufacturer,' *agriment* 'agreement,' *dresmakher* (partial loan translation of *dressmaker*), *istern steyts* 'eastern states,' *dzhabers* 'jobbers,' *kampeyn* 'campaign,' *tenksgiving* 'thanksgiving,' *teks* 'tax,' *polisi* 'policy,' *retayerment* 'retirement,' *kempus* 'campus,' *treyd* 'trade,' *bol-poynt* 'ball-point,' *sayd-layn* 'sideline,' *pensil* 'pencil,' *vazektomi* 'vasectomy,' *tshikn* 'chicken,' *parsli* 'parsley,' *paynepl* 'pineapple.'

One of these terms (*front-liniye*) is covered in Weinreich's dictionary under the individual components, and several are variants of recorded terms (e.g., *kempus* and *kampeyn* are recorded by Weinreich as *kampus* and *kampaniye*). Except for three terms (*vazektomi, dzhabers,* and *bol-poynt*), all have Yiddish equivalents or at least can be rendered in Yiddish without resorting to direct borrowing.[7] Why, then, did the writers of *Forverts* fail to use the established Yiddish terms for such words as pencil, trade, chicken, parsley, and Christmas?

In *Languages in Contact,* Weinreich gives various reasons for lexical borrowing, one of which is the low frequency of certain words in the recipient language.[8] Possibly the standard Yiddish words for pencil, trade, chicken, etc., have become so infrequent among American Yiddish speakers that their English equivalents must be used because they come more easily to mind. Most American Yiddish speakers and writers of today are Yiddish-English bilinguals who probably use Enlgish more frequently than yiddish. This suggests that American Yiddish may be becoming more and more Americanized lexically, gradually replacing established Yiddish words of non-English origin with their English equivalents. Runaway permissivism on the part of Yiddish writers and editors certainly will accelerate the process. On the other hand, the process may possibly be slowed down or reversed through deliberate efforts by language-conscious, cultivated writers and speakers of Yiddish. This could be already happening to some extent.

A comparison of the 1975 issue of *Forverts* with two later

issues, those of May 18 and June 15, 1984, seems to indicate a change in attitude or policy with respect to the admission of Anglicisms into the paper. Perhaps the change is connected with the conversion of the paper into a weekly in 1982, which may have given the editors more time to stylize and edit the articles. In any case, the first ten pages in both issues were free of new English borrowings. In marked contrast, the short news pieces and advertisements in the back pages were filled with Anglicisms of the sort Max Weinreich had no use for: *onderteyker* 'undertaker,' *fyuneral direktor, kongregeyshon* (the standard Yiddish word is *kongregatsiye*), *bilding, lontshen* 'luncheon,' *lobi* 'lobby,' and "potato Yiddish" transliterations of words like *baths, showers, single rooms, dining room, air-conditioned, diets, snacks,* and the like. The obvious conclusion is that the editors printed the copy sent in by advertisers and publicists without attempting to edit them, a state of affairs probably due more to economic considerations than to linguistic insensitivity.

To continue our description of American Yiddish, English loanwords usually take on Yiddish forms, becoming integrated into Yiddish patterns of declension, conjugation, and derivation. In American Yiddish the neuter gender (indicated by the article *dos*) is dropped, and the feminine *di* becomes more productive: *di treyn* 'the train,' *di trok* 'the truck,' instead of *dos* or *der trok*. Adjectives are inflected as in Yiddish (*di nekst-dorike moyd* 'the next-door girl') as are nouns: *der shap* 'the shop' becomes in the plural *di sheper* 'the shops';[9] *forman* 'foreman' becomes *forlayt* in the plural.[10] The Yiddish plural *-es* produces *boyes* from English boy and *kares* from English *car*. From *olrayt* 'all right' American Yiddish derived *olraytnik* 'upstart, parvenu'[11] and the feminine *olraytnitse*; from *holdop* 'holdup' it derived *holdopnik* 'holdup artist'; and from *drayver* 'driver' the feminine *drayverke*. The feminine suffix *-n* also yields *drayvern, titshern* from English *teacher,* *bukipern* from English *bookkeeper.* Among diminutives English *boy* produced *boytshik* and the plural *boytshiklekh*, and *rum* 'room' the diminutive *rumke*. The Yiddish suffix *-ele* is especially productive as an endearing diminutive appended to English given names, e.g., *Stevele, Evele*. Such diminutive names have passed into English use:

> From the geisha girl, Milty, she'll *plotz!* Ha ha! You did it, Miltaleh, and without lifting a finger! (Philip Roth, *Portnoy's Complaint*, 1969, Bantam ed., p. 213).

> It's like going into the store and Herbie asks you what he can get you and you say, "Herbala, open me a can of tuna" (Zero Mostel, *New Yorker*, August 6, 1973, p. 77).

Sometimes the diminutive may appear in disguised form. For example the feminine names *Fredelle* and *Rochelle* turn out to be Anglicizations of Yiddish *Freydele* (diminutive of *Freyde* 'Frieda') and *Rokhele* (diminutive of *Rokhl* 'Rachel').

Groups of English words with the same stem are Yiddishized by altering derivational suffixes: nouns in *-tion* take on the ending *-tsiye*, adjectives in *-ic* the ending *-ish*, nouns in *-ity* the ending *-itet*, and so on, as in *segregatsiye* 'segregation,' *supersonish* 'supersonic,' *aktualitet* 'actuality,' *prefabritsirt* 'prefabricated,' etc. These are standard Yiddish suffixes, of course, used in forms borrowed from other languages besides English.

Similarly English verbs are conjugated with Yiddish forms, taking on *-n* or *-en* in the infinitive and *ge-* in the past participle: *kidnepn* 'to kidnap,' *blofn* 'to bluff,' *straykn* 'to strike,' *troblen* 'to trouble,' *atendn* 'to attend,' *afordn* 'to afford'; *gekidnept* 'kidnapped,' *gebadert* 'bothered,' *gemuft* 'moved to another place,' etc. Common American English verb phrases are taken whole into American Yiddish and reproduced in Yiddish form, as for example *ikh hob getsheyndzht mayn* *maynd* 'I changed my mind,' *er hot geketsht a kold* 'he caught a cold,' *zey veln delivern di gudz* 'they will deliver the goods,' *nemen a vok* 'to take a walk,' *loyfn far ofis* 'to run for office,' *endzhoyen zikh* 'to enjoy oneself.'

Other commonly used phrases patterned on American English include:

makhn a lebn 'to make a living'
aroysgeyn mit a meydl 'to go out with a girl'
gebn kredit far 'to give credit for'
adresirn a farzamlung 'to address a meeting'
oprufn oyfn telefon 'to call up on the telephone'
es nemt tsayt 'it takes time'

Among the significant contributions of English to American Yiddish are numerous loan translations and hybrid compounds. More often than not, these are neologisms created by linguists, writers, and journalists, and should be distinguished from the folk borrowings or adaptations discussed above. For example: *mutertog* 'Mother's Day,' *danktog* 'Thanksgiving Day,' *supermark* 'supermarket,' *fregprogram* 'quiz program,' *kvadrattants* 'square dance,' *kvalpen* 'fountain pen,' *medfarzorg* 'medicare,' *momentbild* 'snapshot.' A number of such coinages are listed by Maurice Samuel in *In Praise of Yiddish* from a longer group attributed by Yudel Mark to Max Weinreich.[12] Among them are *umetumik* 'ubiquitous' (from *umetum* 'everywhere'), *aylsho* 'rush hour,' *dakhdire* 'penthouse,' *kush-vokh* 'honeymoon' (lit., 'kiss-week'), and *omeynzoger* 'yesman' (lit., 'amen-sayer'). All of these were introduced by Uriel Weinreich into his *Modern English-Yiddish Yiddish-English Dictionary*.

Many structural changes in American Yiddish syntax have been traced to the influence of American English. Joffe has detected a preference for the passive construction, citing such phrases as *a miting vet opgehaltn vern* 'a meeting will be held' and *di bikher zaynen oyfgegesn gevorn fun mayz* 'the books were devoured by mice' as illustrations of this tendency. Yudel Mark records many other examples of syntactic modifications on the model of English, only a few of which need to be mentioned here:[13]

Word order: *Kayn mol frier iz er nit geven . . .* 'Never before was he . . .' instead of *Er iz kayn mol . . . .*

Intrusion of preposition: *Ikh ken im far finf yor* 'I know him for five years' (*far* is unnecessary).

Replacement of definite article with pronoun: *Ikh leyg arayn mayn* (instead of *di*) *hent in mayn keshene* 'I put my hand in my pocket.'

The English influence is most clearly manifested in the literal reproduction of idioms. For example:

Dos alts! 'That's all!' (*Dos* 'that' being equated with *that's*)

A fraynd fun mir 'a friend of mine'

azoy lang vi er iz nito 'as long as he is absent' (instead of the Yiddish equivalent *kol-zman er iz nito*)

Es arbet nit 'It doesn't work'

letstn yor 'last year' (instead of *far a yorn*)

letste vokh 'last week' (instead of *farakhtogn*)

Ikh bin kalt 'I am cold' (instead of *Mir iz kalt*)

Finally, a word on the effect of American English on the meanings of both Yiddish words and borrowed English words. The senses of Yiddish words are constantly extended through English influence. Two examples taken from the first issue of *Forverts* mentioned above, *teks-shnitn* 'tax cuts' and *broynen* 'to brown' (in cooking), illustrate this. In the first example *shnitn* 'cuts' is extended in application and in the second the adjective *broyn* 'brown' takes on a verb function (with a corresponding change in form). Well-established semantic extensions are exemplified by *loyfn* 'to run' used in the sense of 'to be a candidate,' on the model of English *run* (for president, etc.); *geyn* 'to go (on foot)' used in the meaning 'to travel,' after English *go* (to Alaska, etc.); *glaykhn* 'to like (someone or something), extended from the standard Yiddish meaning 'to liken, compare' on the model of the English pair *liken: like*; and *shteyn* 'to stand,' extended in meaning to 'to stay' (as in *er shteyt bay mir in hoyz* 'he is staying in my house') under the influence of the somewhat homophonous English verb *stay* (but note also the standard Yiddish verb *aynshteyn* 'to stay at, be lodged').

Borrowings from English may in turn become specialized semantically in American Yiddish. Thus *loyer* 'lawyer' is applied in American Yiddish specifically to an American attorney, whereas the older word, *advokat*, remains the general term for any lawyer. Similarly, *peyper* was transferred from American English *paper* chiefly in the sense of 'newspaper.' Some loanwords acquire meanings not found in English; American Yiddish *payde* 'payday' came to mean 'wages,' a sense which American English *payday* never had.[14] Likewise, American Yiddish *nekst* 'next,' assuming the function of a noun, acquired the meaning 'turn,' as in *s' iz mayn nekst* 'it's my turn.'

In sum, the influence of American English on the Yiddish language has been—and continues to be—extensive. Even the Yiddish of the ultrareligious has been affected.[15] Still, the work of Yiddish language standardizers and normativists to stem the tide of Anglicisms flooding the standard language has been steadily gaining ground. At least in writing one encounters ever greater avoidance of obvious Americanisms. But the speech of most Americans who talk Yiddish is still heavily laced with Anglicisms. Yiddish speakers from other countries, though managing to communicate in Yiddish with their American counterparts, often do not understand clearly what the latter say and are at first stumped by the high frequency of Anglicisms in American Yiddish. When an American Yiddish speaker utters a sentence like *Ikh vil stapn oyfn koner tsu koyfn a peyper* 'I want to stop at the corner to buy a paper,' it often seems to a Yiddish speaker from Russia or Israel that he is listening to a badly mangled Yiddish. Yet while the foreign Yiddish speaker will wince at sentences like these, it will probably amuse him to discover that there is another facet to the intimate relationship between Yiddish and English—English words and phrases that sound like Yiddish.

The Yiddish Influence
on English

5

Before the nineteenth century we find no Yiddish-origin words recorded in the English language. Words and names of Hebrew origin were of course long ago established in English (many as far back as Old English) due to the influence of Bible translations: *camel, manna, jot, jubilee, cherub, amen, gehenna, leviathan, behemoth, shekel, shibboleth,* and others. Through the work of English Renaissance scholars a considerable number of religio-cultural terms were also borrowed from Hebrew, words such as *Cabbala* (1521), *Talmud* (1532), *Sanhedrin* (1588), *Mishnah* (1610), and *mezuzah* (1650). But there is no evidence of Yiddish-derived words occurring in English writings before the 1800s.

Jews had lived in the British Isles as far back as the Norman Conquest (1066), and apparently lived there peacefully until the Third Crusade and the accession of Richard I (both in 1189), when anti-Jewish riots broke out, followed by oppressive extortionary measures against the Jewish population that lasted until 1290. On November 30th of that year Edward I, yielding to the demands of the clergy and the baronage, expelled the 16,000 Jews of England. It was not until three and a half centuries later, in the 1650s, that a post-Reformation awakening of interest in Jews and Judaism led to the readmission of the Jews. But a century later the Jewish population of

Great Britain was still numerically small and isolated, with little opportunity to introduce new Hebrew or Yiddish words into the English vocabulary of the era.

A similar situation existed in the New World. The first Jews (of Spanish-Portuguese origin) had arrived in New Amsterdam in 1654, followed by others when the English replaced the Dutch ten years later. But up until the American Revolution there were only about 2,500 Jews in the Colonies; not until the 1850s did Jews begin to settle in the United States in sufficient numbers to make their presence and influence felt. As a result of the post-Napoleonic revolutionary ferment in Europe, especially Germany, emigration to the United States increased its Jewish population between 1850 and 1870 from 50,000 to 250,000. In the same period, the Jewish population of Great Britain rose from 35,000 to about 50,000.

It was in this period that Yiddish words began to trickle into English on both sides of the Atlantic. Some of the best known Yiddish-origin words first recorded in English at this time are *kosher* 'ritually fit,' its antonym *treyf* (both first recorded in 1851), and *bar mitsve* 'boy of thirteen who attains his religious majority' (1861).[1] It should be noted, though, that these and other religio-cultural terms used by Yiddish speakers had corresponding Judezmo forms used by Sephardic (Spanish-origin) Jews who had settled in the United States since the 1600s, so that there was probably considerable overlap; at least in early documents it is not always clear whether a particular Jewish word is of immediate Hebrew, Judezmo, or Yiddish origin. Thus the term *Talmud Torah* 'Jewish religious school,' appearing in the constitution and regulations of a Jewish school in New York City in 1808, could as easily have been taken from Judezmo as from Yiddish.[2] The same can be said for the names of the Jewish New Year and the Day of Atonement, which appear in the forms *Rosh Ha-Shanah* and *Yom Kippur* in an English letter dated 1791, written by Rebecca Samuels, the wife of a Virginia silversmith.[3] In view of the undoubtedly very early use of such terms among American Sephardic Jews, it is probably safest to assume that these terms predated (but were later reinforced by) the arrival of Yiddish speakers to the United States.

Another early Yiddishism in English was *ganef* 'thief,' recorded in the OED from 1852 (in Dickens' *Bleak House*). But Partridge, in *A Dictionary of the Underworld*, cites the form *gonnof* in the sense of 'a thief' as having been recorded by H. Brandon in *Poverty, Mendacity, and Crime* in 1839.[4] The next date in Partridge is 1845, from the *National Police Gazette*, an American periodical. These early references to *ganef* in disreputable contexts suggest that the word (and probably other Yiddishisms used in the underworld) came into American English not through the speech of Jewish immigrants but via the cant or argot of international thieves.[5] Two authorities on underworld slang, David Maurer and Gerald Cohen, point out that the *gun* in *gun-moll* and in *son-of-a-gun* derive from the criminal slang term *gun* 'thief' (more narrowly, 'pickpocket'), which in turn derives by shortening from *ganef*.[6] Similarly, the common Yiddishism *goy* 'non-Jew' is first attested in an English source (*Tait's Edinburgh Magazine*) in 1835, and this earliest use is in the argot of criminals called crimps who entrapped or forced men into service as sailors.[7]

According to Mencken, a number of Yiddish terms were brought into this country by German (presumably Gentile) speakers even before Yiddish became one of the principal languages of New York, and he cites as examples *ganef*, *kosher*, *meshuge* 'crazy,' *mazuma* 'money, cash,' *shekels* 'money,' and *tokhes* 'backside.' Mencken states that all of these words were used by German schoolmasters in Baltimore in the 1880s.[8] This is quite possible, since it is well known that modern German, like Dutch, appropriated numerous Yiddishisms that are still part of its colloquial stock. Nevertheless, these early uses in English were only vague intimations of the flood that would ensue with the arrival of the Jewish immigrants.

As was pointed out earlier, the seminal contact between Yiddish and English occurred in the 1880s. With hundreds of thousands of Jewish immigrants from Russia and Rumania pouring into this country, and tens of thousands into England (where by 1917 the Jewish population rose to 250,000), Yiddish words mixed with English became a familiar sound to New Yorkers and Londoners alike. In New York City, the Lower East Side became the populous center from which the Yiddish language and culture emanated; in England, the East End of London, with its own large concentration of immigrant Jews, came to occupy a similar central position in the dissemination of Yiddish.

It was to the East End that the Anglo-Jewish writer Israel Zangwill applied in 1892 the word *ghetto,* thereby adding to the infamous old word the new sense of 'a city quarter inhabited by poor immigrant Jews.' Through books and plays dealing with life in the East End (*Children of the Ghetto,* 1892; *Ghetto Tragedies* and *Ghetto Comedies,* both 1894; *Dreamers of the Ghetto,* 1898; *The Melting Pot,* 1908; and many others), Zangwill popularized in English a number of Yiddish words, such as *shnorer* 'beggar,' *shlemiel* 'clumsy, bungling person,' *goye* 'Gentile woman,' *gefilte fish* 'stuffed boneless cake of fish,' *tales* 'prayer shawl,' *shoykhet* 'Jewish slaughterer,' *shames* 'synagogue beadle,' *shul* 'synagogue,' and *kadish* 'mourner's prayer.' Some of these terms appeared in English publications occasionally before Zangwill, as for example *shul,* cited in the 1873 edition of *The Slang Dictionary* (originally published in 1859 by "A London Antiquary" under the title *The Dictionary of Modern Slang, Cant, and Vulgar Words*).

A British lexicographer of the early 1900s, J. Redding Ware, described the setting of the new Yiddish words:

In the East [of London] the confusion of languages is a world of 'variants'—there must be half-a-dozen of Anglo-Yiddish alone—all, however, outgrown from the Hebrew stem.[9]

The 'variants' Ware referred to were the variety of pronunciations heard in the East End, representing the various Eastern Yiddish dialects reflected in such Anglicized spellings of that period as *tryfer, trefa, tripha, terefah* for the Yiddish word *treyfe,* meaning 'non-kosher food.'

Some years before Zangwill wrote his popular novels about the East End, the British public had already had an exposure to modern Jewish life in George Eliot's famous book about Zionism, *Daniel Deronda* (1876). Though the Jewish setting of the novel is Germany rather than London, Eliot introduces many Jewish concepts and along with them Jewish (Yiddish and Hebrew) terms:

> The white *talithim* had mustered, the reader had mounted to the *almemor* or platform, and the service began (*Daniel Deronda,* IV, 32, p. 274).

> If your mother had lived, she would have forgiven me—thirty-four years ago I put the ring on her finger under the Chuppa, and we were made one (*Daniel Deronda,* VIII, 66, p. 586).

(*talithim* represents Yiddish *taleysim* 'prayer shawls'; *chuppa* represents Yiddish *khupe* 'wedding canopy'; *almemor* came from Hebrew and ultimately from Arabic *al-minbar* 'the platform')

Among the many English words adopted from Yiddish during the 1890s were the word *Yiddish* itself (1886 in the OED) and *Yid* (1890). The latter is erroneously defined in the OED as "A Jew who speaks Yiddish" and also wrongly etymologized as a back formation from the word *Yiddish. Yid* actually means 'a Jew' and comes from the Yiddish word with the same meaning. The term, incidentally, is derogatory in English (though not of course in Yiddish):

> And only Pound, of these writers, uses, in his poetry, words like "yid" and "kike" (Cyril Conolly, London *Sunday Times,* September 21, 1966).

Another common word of Yiddish origin that became naturalized in American English is the verb *kibitz,* which surprisingly enough was not recorded until the late 1920s. The first printed record of *kibitzing* is found in *Lighting Fixtures and Lighting,* the trade journal of the American lighting industry, which in its issue of February 1927 devoted an editorial to this word, defining it as a slang expression used to indicate the act of offering gratuitous advice by an outsider. "Kibbitzers [sic] are out in full force at the fixture shows," the editorial remarked.[13] In the thirties and forties the word became common currency in American English and by now it is not generally regarded as a Yiddishism, though it is still used mostly colloquially, and sometimes thought of as slang.

After the 1930s the use of Yiddish as a primary language declined in the United States and Great Britain. Cultural assimilation of the Jews in Britain and such adverse conditions in this country as Americanization policies, anti-immigration policies, the economic havoc of the depression—all played their part in accelerating the decline of such institutions as the Yiddish theater, Yiddish press, Yiddish culture schools, and the Yiddish language. Children in Jewish parochial schools were being taught almost exclusively in English, and English-language newspapers and magazines of the Jewish community began to fill the vacuum left by the demise of Yiddish publications. Yet it was this period that marked the entry of a great many Yiddish words into American English, for the Yiddish language, though no longer widely spoken, was still known to millions of American Jews and the introduction of familiar

Yiddish words into English came naturally to those who knew or remembered them with fondness or nostalgia.

Nicholas I was a passionate anti-semite, determined to eliminate the 'Zhyds' (Yids) (A. J. P. Taylor, *New Statesman*, January 31, 1975, p. 149).

There was no one of the stature of a Zangwill or a George Eliot in the United States during the latter part of the 1800s, hence the record of Yiddishisms entering American English does not begin until after the turn of the century. Yet there can be no doubt that New York's East Side, with a far larger Jewish population than the East End of London, had at least as great a share in the introduction of Yiddish loans into English as did its British counterpart; it is merely by historical accident that an early chronicler of immigrant life of Zangwill's popularity was born in England instead of America. Not until 1917 did the first important and influential book written in English and dealing with Jewish life in America appear: Abraham Cahan's *The Rise of David Levinsky*. Cahan, best known as the editor of the Yiddish daily *Forverts,* had earlier written other books in English about the New York ghetto, but these works of fiction never reached as large an audience as this novel.[10] Although *The Rise of David Levinsky* contains a number of Yiddishisms (e.g., *kheyder* 'traditional Jewish elementary school,' *Reb,* form of address for a man), by the time of its appearance in the second decade of the century the Yiddishisms he used were well known in New York, Chicago, and other American cities where immigrant Jews had settled in large numbers after the 1890s.

The record of the introduction of Yiddish into American English is thus rather poor. The earliest Yiddish loan to American English (as opposed to British English) appears to be the slangism *mazuma* 'money, cash' (from Yiddish *mezumen* 'cash'), recorded as *mazume* in the OED Supplement (Vol. II, 1976) in the following 1904 citation:

We're a sad bunch . . . when we haven't a little mazume in the
vest pocket (G. V. Hobart, *Jim Hickey*, 1.15).[11]

Mazuma has been in continuous use since then. It was used by
O. Henry in 1906, by Jack London in *Smoke Bellew* (1912),
Sinclair Lewis in *Main Street* (1920), and Carl Sandburg in
Smoke and Steel (1920); yet, like many words taken from
Yiddish, it has never gained admission into formal English and
is still regarded as slang.

Among other early Yiddish entries into American English is
goy, used by Sinclair Lewis in his novel *The Job* (1916), and
shlemiel, attested in Mitford Mathews' *A Dictionary of Americanisms* (Chicago: The University of Chicago Press, 1951)
with a 1919 citation from an American English-Jewish periodical, the *San Francisco Hebrew*. The origin of Yiddish
shlemiel is somewhat obscure. According to Mathews,
shlemiel apparently came from "[Adalbert von] Chamisso's
well-known story, *Peter Schlemihl*, of the unfortunate wretch
who sold his shadow to the devil." However, it is very unlikely
that the English word came from this source, since its first
appearance is as a Yiddish-origin word in Zangwill's *Children
of the Ghetto*; besides, this Western Yiddish word is far older
than Chamisso's story, which appeared in 1814. More probably, Chamisso took the name of his hero from the Yiddish
word; accordingly *Webster's Third* and the OED Supplement
trace the word to Yiddish and ultimately to the Biblical name
of *Shelumiel* (Numbers 1:6), "said by the Talmud to have met
with an unhappy end" (OED Supplement, Vol. III, 1982).[12]

This, too, was the period when a new generation of American-born Jewish writers sprang up, writing novels and stories
in English which often included Yiddishisms they had picked
up in childhood and used themselves. Among them were such
popular authors as Edna Ferber, Fannie Hurst, Anzia
Yezierska, Ludwig Lewisohn, Michael Gold, Henry Roth, and
Ben Hecht, followed by a younger generation of writers such

as Meyer Levin, Myron Brinig, Jerome Weidman, Irwin Shaw, Saul Bellow, Bernard Malamud, Norman Mailer, Herman Wouk, Philip Roth, Chaim Potok, and E. L. Doctorow. Well-known Jewish-American humorists also had a large share in the popularization of Yiddishisms, among them Arthur Kober, Milt Gross, Sam Levenson, Harry Golden, Jack Benny, George Burns, Milton Berle, Sid Cesar, Woody Allen, and many others. In recent years the translated works of contemporary Yiddish writers, notably the Nobel Prize-winning novelist Isaac Bashevis Singer and the poet and novelist Chaim Grade, have helped keep Yiddish-origin words alive in English.

By the 1930s, the Yiddish-origin words recorded by Mencken in *The American Language* were quite well known to a large number of non-Jewish Americans. Some of these words became thoroughly established in American English, so much so that they began to undergo various phonetic, grammatical, and semantic developments. Among such naturalized words were *kosher, shamus, bagel,* and *lox.*

Kosher, which was originally adopted as an adjective meaning 'ritually fit, lawful,' was also borrowed from Western Yiddish as a verb meaning 'to make (meat) kosher.' The OED cites Zangwill's use of this verb in 1892:

She . . . would never fail to light the Sabbath candles nor to kosher the meat (*Children of the Ghetto,* viii, 83).

The Eastern Yiddish equivalent of this verb, *kashern,* was in turn taken into English as a variant of the verb *kosher,* thus:

Muslim dietary rules resemble the Jewish ones, but there are no professional priests or rabbis to kasher (*Atlantic,* July 1959, p. 94).

In turn the adjective *kosher* was reborrowed from Yiddish in the general sense of 'all right, acceptable, reliable, satisfactory, legitimate,' a sense that is found originally in Yiddish (and in Hebrew *kasher*) and not, as has been contended, a figurative use of English *kosher* (supposedly spread by rum runners during Prohibition). In English slang this sense is first attested in 1896, in Farmer and Henley's *A Dictionary of Slang and Its Analogues* (published 1890–1904), where it is labeled "common" and defined as 'fair, square.' Here are two later examples of this use:

> Now, the fateful question of whether baseball's contracts and agreements are kosher is back before the top court (*Newsweek*, October 26, 1953, p. 98).

> We had a dandy hassle proving I was kosher, but he finally let me upstairs (S. J. Perelman, *New Yorker*, January 28, 1961, p. 29).

Shamus 'a policeman or detective' is most familiar to readers of American whodunits, where the term first began to appear in the 1930s. Its appearance in detective stories probably reflects earlier criminal use. According to Maurer, *shamus* meant 'store detective' to a passer of counterfeit money, and 'policeman' to a pickpocket.[14] Goldin records the meaning 'guard; any prison guard' among prisoners.[15] Its meanings are purely American, but the word is traced back to Yiddish *shames* 'a synagogue caretaker or watchman, a beadle,' perhaps, as *Webster's Third* suggests, "from a jocular suggestion of similarity between the duties of a sexton and those of a house detective in a department store." However, the word has been chiefly associated in general slang with the type of tough private eye popularized by Raymond Chandler:

> Chandler's shamus—forever ploughing into the heart of trouble, a sucker, at heart, for a dame in distress—represents the wish-fulfillment of an ideal not yet quite dead (Charles J. Rolo, "Simenon and Spillane," *New World Writing*, April 1952, p. 241).

Nick Marshall, London shamus, in pickle when client he never saw turns up dead in shabby hotel (*Saturday Review*, February 27, 1960, p. 32).

Although the phrase "bagels and lox" is peculiarly suggestive of Jewish eating habits, the words *bagel* and *lox* have become fully established terms in American English. The OED Supplement (Vol. I, 1972) attests *bagel* since 1932, but cites sources for its earlier variant *beigel* since 1919, and precedes the latter with a much earlier, bracketed citation from Zangwill (*Children of the Ghetto*, 1892), who uses the somewhat Germanized spelling *Beuglich* to render the Yiddish plural form *beyglekh*. It is not far-fetched to assume that *bagel* (however it may be spelled) has been in continuous use in English since the nineteenth century, despite the lack of adequate evidence to prove this.

Lox 'a salty variety of smoked salmon' is chiefly of interest in that it has an English cognate, *lax* 'salmon,' which existed in Old and Middle English, dropped partly out of use about the 1600s, and was apparently reborrowed in the early 1800s from Norwegian *laks*. The cognate Yiddish word *laks* yielded American English *lox*. The spelling *lax* is now rarely encountered. Certainly Americans use the word *salmon*, not *lax*. But when they mean the salty variety of salmon, as distinguished from the bland Nova Scotia type, they ask for lox:

He [Arthur Goldberg] followed this up, a few days after his induction, with a Sunday-morning brunch at his house for his fellow Cabinet members, at which he introduced them to the delights of scrambled eggs with bagels and lox (Robert Shaplen, *New Yorker*, April 14, 1962, p. 68).

A similar doubling of native English and native Yiddish forms occurs in the word *mish-mash*. This reduplication has been recorded in English since 1585, but the last citation for it in the OED is, curiously, from *Daniel Deronda*:

A ridiculous mish-mash of superannuated customs and false
ambition (XXII, p. 22).

It is a moot question whether Eliot's use of this word in her
"Jewish" book was influenced by the Yiddish near-homo-
phone (also in German as *Mischmasch,* a word adopted by
Lewis Carroll for a title circa 1855). In recent years it appears
that the Yiddish word (often misspelled as *mish-mosh*) has
more or less blended with the English one:

> It takes considerable experience to put a mish-mosh together
> and have it come off as anything but a mish-mosh (Nan Ick-
> eringill, *New York Times,* August 26, 1966, p. 39).

Jewish cookery is an area of Yiddish usage which has provided English with quite a number of terms, e.g., *kishke*
'stuffed derma' (1936), *blintse* 'rolled pancake' (1903), *latke*
'potato pancake' (1927), *knish* 'kind of dumpling' (1930),
kugl 'noodle or potato pudding' (1846!), *lokshn* 'noodles'
(1892), *farfl* 'pellets of noodle dough' (1892, Zangwill). More
recent terms (chiefly since the 1940s and 1950s) include
flanken 'cooked flank of beef,' *matzo ball* 'round dumpling
made with matzo meal,' *bialy* 'kind of flat onion roll,' and
many others.

The term *borsht,* misspelled as *borscht,* is treated by current
dictionaries as a variant of the form *borsch,* which is derived
from Russian *borshch.*[16] The fact, however, is that *borsht* and
borsch have different spellings, pronunciations, meanings, and
origins, and should therefore be treated separately rather than
as variants. The form *borsch* is indeed from the Russian (attested in English since 1884) and means a Russian soup made
with vegetables and meat stock. But *borsht* comes from Yiddish (which in turn came from a Slavic, not necessarily Russian, form of the word) and it usually means a soup made with
beets. The Yiddish origin of *borsht* should not be ignored,
especially since it is what accounts for the terms *borsht belt*

and *borsht circuit,* referring to the variety shows provided in the Jewish summer resorts in the Catskills:

> That same year, 1949, he [Eddie Fisher] also sang with the band at Grossinger's, richest soup stock on the Borscht circuit (*Newsweek,* April 20, 1953, p. 92).

During the 1920s and 1930s no one did more to record the Yiddishisms that had seeped into American English than H. L. Mencken. He was supplied with much of his material about Yiddish by the editor of the *Forverts,* Abraham Cahan. Most of the Yiddish loanwords recorded by Mencken in the various editions of *The American Language* (1919, 1921, 1923, 1936) and in its two Supplements (1945, 1948) are still widely used in the United States (as well as in Canada and Great Britain, and to some extent in Australia and South Africa). What is especially noteworthy about Mencken's work in this area is the pains he took to give the narrowest possible definitions to the terms he encountered, thereby providing us with a fascinating glimpse of the early uses of Yiddish loanwords in American English. Instead of simply translating the loanwords, he chose to show the specific or contextual uses of the words in English.

Thus, for example, Mencken places the form *shmoosing* under the heading "Garment Workers" and defines it as 'Idling around and talking shop.'[17] Of course the Yiddish-derived verb *shmus* simply means 'to chat,' and chatting is what the garment workers were doing. The verb is attested in the OED Supplement (Vol. III, 1982) since 1897 (in *The New York Times Weekly*), and the noun in the sense of 'a chat' is recorded since 1939. The following examples of the word's use show its general application. Note the variant spellings, the second probably representing a Western Yiddish pronunciation[18]:

> "I've been dressing and shmoosing," said Simon. "There's plenty of time—what's the big rush?" (Saul Bellow, *The Adventures of Augie March,* 1949, Compass Books ed., p. 241).

William H. Whyte, he wrote "The Organization Man," is an expert on schmoozing. . . . One thing he has discovered is where people schmooze. . . . A popular place to schmooze, he said, is the southeast corner of 50th Street and Fifth Avenue (John Corry, *New York Times,* March 1, 1974).

Under the heading "Installment House Salesman" Mencken records "*schlepp,* v. To move furniture about on the sales floor."[19] Today the verb *shlep* means simply 'to drag,' as in:

I shlepped those bulbs around For two months from place to place, looking for a home, All that winter (Edward Field, *New Yorker,* April 27, 1963, p. 47).

This is the sense in which Joyce used the word in *Ulysses:*

She trudges, schlepps, trains, drags . . . her load (James Joyce, *Ulysses,* 1922, p. 48).

The idiom *shlep around* is a partial loan translation of Yiddish *arumshlepn* meaning 'to run around':

"Charlotte Ford Niarchos," she [society columnist Suzi] wrote in her first column, "has been schlepping around the Greek Islands with her ex-husband" (*Time,* June 30, 1967, p. 48).

The nouns *shlep* (literally 'a pull, a drag' in Yiddish) and *shleper* (literally 'one who drags' in Yiddish) both mean 'a clod, bore, drag':

Death was just here. . . . In person. Or somebody who claims to be Death. But, Moe, he's such a *schlep!* (Woody Allen, *New Yorker,* July 27, 1968, p. 33).

But the sun shines on everybody, on the Princess Schaumburg Lippe of Austria and some schlepper from Syosset (Horace Sutton, *Saturday Review,* January 1, 1966, p. 43).

There is today, in addition, the English derivative *shleppy* 'bedraggled' (with no corresponding Yiddish form):

> In the first scene, we are asked to believe that a wealthy New York housewife (Fawcett-Majors) would fall instantly in love with a shleppy Macy's salesman (Jeff Bridges) she spots across a crowded store (*Time*, October 9, 1978, p. 101).

Under the heading "Shoe Clerks" Mencken defines the American slangism *schlock* as 'an overcharge.'[20] The meaning Mencken assigns to the word seems considerably removed from both its common meaning, 'a cheap or inferior product, junk' (recorded in the OED Supplement, III, 1982, from 1915), and the sense of the Yiddish word *shlak* 'a stroke, an evil, a nuisance,' which is thought to be its source. In *The Taste of Yiddish* Feinsilver suggests that there may be as many as three Yiddish words, *shlak, shlakht,* 'slaughter,' and *shlogn* 'to hit,' involved in the etymology of *schlock,* a suggestion tentatively approved by David Gold in *Comments on Etymology.*[21] Yet in the particular meaning of 'an overcharge' (though possibly there may be some semantic thread running between the Yiddish sense of 'a nuisance' and that of 'an overcharge'), one cannot help thinking that perhaps Mencken misinterpreted the meaning of *schlock* as used by shoe clerks. Perhaps, since he knew German, he connected the word with *Schlag,* as in *Zuschlag* 'surcharge, supplementary fee.' Being unfamiliar with Yiddish he sometimes missed certain subtleties of the language. For example, he records under "Garment Workers" the term *balmechule,* defining it as 'a slow and inferior worker,'[22] and noting that the term came from "Yiddish *mechulle* [*mekhule*] spoiled, out of order, bankrupt," all of which is true enough. What he failed to recognize is that the word was a slangy pun on the standard Yiddish word *balmelokhe* (or better, on its Central Yiddish dialectal variant, *balmelukhe*), meaning 'a craftsman, a skilled worker,' or exactly the opposite of what Mencken's *balmechule* was.

Many of the spellings of Yiddish loanwords given by Mencken have changed over the years, though generally not enough to go unrecognized. The only exception seems to be *dokus* 'backside, buttocks.' In his Supplement I (1945, p. 433) Mencken updated the spelling to *tochos,* adding still other variants: *tokos, tokus, tochus.* These later spellings reflect the standard Yiddish pronunciation of the word, *tokhes,* while the earlier *dokus* was borrowed from regional Western Yiddish *dokhes* (which was also borrowed by some German dialects in the forms *Doches, Dokes,* so possibly German influence may also be involved in the etymology of *dokus*).[23] Because the word is a vulgarism (both in English and Yiddish, even though in Yiddish it was originally a euphemism based on the Hebrew word meaning 'under, below'), it has taken on a startling pronunciation and spelling change since the 1960s. The new form, *tushie* or *tushy,* was apparently a "baby-talk" diminutive formed from *tukhes* (from the Southeastern Yiddish variant of Northeastern and standard Yiddish *tokhes*) on the analogy of such English diminutive forms as *tummy* and *footsie.* The new form caught on as an acceptable slang replacement of the vulgar forms:

> Reaching for the surefire laugh that any Yiddishism provokes in New York, Miss Channing is obliged to pronounce "touchée" as "tushy" (Brendan Gill, *New Yorker,* February 4, 1974, p. 46).

The word has been further shortened to *tush,* as in the Mel Brooks film *Blazing Saddles,* where it is made to rhyme with *push* in a song.

Few American slang vulgarisms of Yiddish origin were recorded by Mencken, mostly because they occurred usually in speech rather than in writing and did not appear in popular novels and elsewhere until the ban on obscenities (often self-imposed) in American literature began to lift in the 1940s.

Several Yiddish-origin taboo words are discussed in a 1943 article by Julius Rothenberg in *American Speech,* including *futz* (especially in the verb phrase *futz around,* part translation of Yiddish *arumfartsn*), *pisher,* extended from the colloquial figurative Yiddish sense of 'a young child' to the sense of 'someone stupid or ineffectual,' and the vulgar abbreviation *A.K.* for Yiddish *alter kaker.*[24] Other Yiddish-derived abbreviations, not all scatological or off-color, surfaced in the 1940s. In a 1948 *Miscellany* piece in *American Speech,*[25] Donn O'Meara listed as "alphabetical expressions . . . in use at present among Jewish Americans both Yiddish speaking and otherwise," the abbreviations *A.K., F.A.* for (according to O'Meara) "farshtunkene armpits," *L.M.G.* for Yiddish *lomir geyn* 'let's go,' *T.L.* for Yiddish *tokhes leker* (lit., 'buttocks licker,' i.e., sycophant),[26] and *T.O.T.* for Yiddish *tokhes oyfn tish* (lit., 'buttocks on the table,' i.e., cash on the line).

A humorous aspect of the contact between Yiddish and English that Feinsilver, Rosten, and others have made much of is the so-called bilingual pun, which, according to Feinsilver, "epitomizes . . . the bicultural nature of Jewish existence."[27] Over the years Feinsilver has collected scores of examples from a variety of American English sources. Typical examples she lists are the names of restaurants, such as *Bagel Delox* and (with Italian cuisine) *Kosher Nostra,* proper names like *Tyrannotsores Rex* (play on *tsores* 'trouble') and a ship called *S. S. Mayn Kind* (play on Yiddish *es es mayn kind* 'eat, eat, my child'). Rosten cites a *Phudnik,* which he defines as a "nudnik with a PhD," a writer for *Book Digest* describes the comedian Woody Allen as a "shy shleprechaun,"[28] *Time* magazine, in a review of a book by Peter DeVries, writes that "the beauty of a pun is in the *oy* of the beholder" (play on *oy* 'oh, dear'),[29] and the columnist William Safire puns that President Reagan's aide Ed Meese is "a useful White House counselor—no *mieskeit,* he" (*mieskayt* 'ugly person').[30]

By the 1930s many Yiddish loanwords were well known in

American English slang: words like *makher* 'big operator, bigwig' (recorded in 1930 in *American Speech*), *patsh* 'to slap or smack,' found as early as 1892 in Zangwill ("My mother potched [*sic*] my face"), and *nu* 'so, well,' also found in Zangwill though not attested in American English until 1945. But the 1940s saw the influx of many more Yiddishisms into American English slang, due in large part to the close contact between Jewish and non-Jewish servicemen during World War II. The oral use of these words was not recorded during the war, but it can be taken for granted that the earliest printed dates were preceded by at least several years of oral use among bilingual Jews of the second generation and their Gentile friends. The earliest recorded dates of the following common slang words illustrate the trend: *nebbish* [properly *nebish*] 'ineffectual or unfortunate person, sad sack' (1941, in Bud Schulberg's *What Makes Sammy Run?*, also the short form *neb*), *shnoz* 'nose' (1942, probably a blend of *shnuk* 'snout' and *noz* 'nose'), *shmendrik* 'insignificant person, nobody' (1944), *chutzpah* [properly *khutspe*] 'impertinence, gall' (1945), *shmo* 'simpleton, nitwit' (1947), *shlemazl* 'unlucky person' (1948), *shnuk* 'dope, fool' (1949), *shlump* 'sloppy person' (1952), *mentsh* 'decent person' (1953), *megillah* [preferably *megile*] 'long story' (1957), *yente* 'gossipy woman' (1957).

The period of World War II also gave fresh impetus to the use of Yiddish with the arrival of over two hundred thousand new Jewish immigrants into the United States from various parts of Europe, a great many of them Yiddish speakers. If the reservoir of Yiddish had been drying up in this country, the new arrivals came just in time to replenish it. Unlike their immigrant predecessors of the early part of the century, the newcomers were generally highly educated both in Jewish and secular knowledge and strongly motivated by a desire to preserve the Jewish religion and other aspects of Jewish culture. Their efforts led to the creation of many yeshivas and other educational and social institutions where Yiddish and Hebrew were used along with English, with the result of reinforcing the contact between these languages. The prestige of Hebrew, as the revived modern language of Israel, caused many Yiddishisms in English to be respelled on the Hebrew model: not *Shabes* 'Sabbath' but *Shabbat,* not *sholem* 'peace' (a greeting) but *shalom.* New Hebraisms began to enter English (*kibbutz, hora, sabra, aliya,* etc.) to take their place beside the older Yiddish-origin words.

Still, Yiddishisms continued to enter American slang through the fifties well into the next decade and a half. Once again, the record of dates of earliest attestation of some common Yiddishisms indicates the steady influx: *nash* 'nibble' (1955), *bobkes* 'chicken feed, nothing' (1958), *shvartse(r)* 'black person' (1961), *shmir* 'bribery, flattery' (1961), *kvetsh* 'complain' (1964), *klutz* [properly *klots*] 'clumsy person' (1965), *tsimes* 'big deal, fuss' (1965), *maven* [properly *meyvn*] 'expert, connoisseur' (1965), *shtik* 'act, routine, bit' (1965), *yold* 'dupe, fool' (1966), *zaftik* 'plump, buxom' (1966), *kvel* 'be delighted' (1966), *heymish* 'homey, cozy' (1966), *fonfe* 'to hem and haw' (1968), *khazeray* 'filth, trashy food' (1969). Other Yiddishisms that have become common in American English since the 1960s include *nakhes* 'pride and joy,' *tsores* 'trouble,' *kokhlefl* 'busybody, meddler,' *ay-ay-ay* 'wonderful, terrific,' *tshatshke* or *tsatske* 'toy, trinket, gadget,' *mamzer* 'rascal, rogue.'

The following quotations illustrate the use of some of these words:

> City officials have greeted the revenue-sharing legislation with muted joy—because there is, so far as the city is concerned, both *tsuris* and *naches* in the legislation (William E. Farrell, *New York Times,* Week in Review, October 22, 1972, p. 6).

> Her [Nancy Walker's] face became familiar on the TV tube as . . . Rhoda's *kochleffel* mother (Helen Dorsey, *New York Sunday News,* Sec. 3, January 11, 1976, p. 1).

There are also a substantial number of us whose heads are not so ay-ay-ay (*Harper's,* April 1980, p. 81).

The cupboards . . . reveal a hoard of oddments and *chatchkes*: vanity sets, inlaid boxes, tarnished trays (*Time,* January 2, 1981, p. 61).

"Décor doesn't add to the glamour of a suit," an owner pointed out. "You're not buying the rugs or the lamps or the tsatskes" (Georgia Dulles, *New York Times,* July 12, 1974, p. 31).

"Goniff!" Max screams. "Felon! Mommser! You sold my *vigorish!*" (Roger Angell, *New Yorker,* February 11, 1980, p. 102).

The word now usually spelled *chutzpah* [properly *khutspe*], meaning 'impudence, gall,' and also 'audacity, daring,' became extremely common in the 1960s, although it has been used in American English since the 1940s. The Supplement to the OED (Vol. I, 1972) attests its use since 1945 but as usual, is able to cite Zangwill (who spells it *Chutzbah*) as its earliest attested user in English, in 1892. From 1945 the Supplement jumps to 1967. There is, however, evidence of the word's use in the 1950s, as in the following:

He has *hutzpa,* says Rodzinski, and illustrates what he means with the story of how Bernstein, a mere 35, dared to conduct Beethoven's sacrosanct *Ninth Symphony* with the great Santa Cecilia chorus in Rome. "And he had the nerve to move his hips in time to the music. *Hutzpa!*" (*Time,* February 4, 1957, p. 69).

Theatrical *chutzpa* of a more shameless kind is displayed by Sig Arno (Kenneth Tynan, *New Yorker,* December 20, 1958, p. 65).

"That's a helluva chuzpah," said Gruber (Bernard Malamud, *The Magic Barrel,* 1958, Pocket Book ed., p. 27).

This loanword underwent a shift of meaning in English. In Yiddish, *khutspe* has only a negative meaning, that of 'brazen effrontery or impudence.' Probably influenced by the synonymous English word *nerve,* which can be both negative ("You have some nerve!") and positive ("You got to have nerve to get on in the world"), the loanword acquired in English an additional positive meaning, that of 'great boldness or daring,' as in the following quotations:

> Dr. Shulman's most outstanding quality is *chutzpah*—a combination of enormous self-confidence and indifference to what other people think (Jocelyn Dingman, *Maclean's,* November 5, 1966, p. 67).

> "He has the chutzpah to claim that he had the chutzpah to sneak into the White House and lunch with Reagan" (Jeff Wells, *New York Post,* October 12, 1981, p. 10).

A similar shift in meaning probably occurred with the word usually spelled *glitch,* meaning 'a mishap or malfunction,' whose apparent Yiddish etymon, *glitsh,* has only the literal meaning of 'a slip' (as on the street). Here, again, the catalyst of change appears to have been an English word, the colloquialism *slip-up,* whose meaning is close to that of *glitch.*
   If *glitch* indeed originated from Yiddish, it is a rather unusual loan in that it came into English about 1960 through technological jargon. Used originally in electronics in the sense of an irregularity in voltage, it was adopted by aerospace engineers and expanded to mean any foul-up, anomaly, or mistake. For example:

> They dealt with every imaginable glitch, from premature starts of the camera to unprogrammed movements of the scan platform that was designed to pick up the planet and tell the TV camera when to start functioning (*Time,* July 23, 1965, p. 30).

By the 1970s *glitch* was also used in computer programming, engineering, and astronomy, both as a noun and a verb, and it produced a derivative, *glitchy*:

> In the May 4 *Nature* John Gribbin of *Nature* and Stephen Plagemann of the NASA Institute for Space studies in New York call the occurrence a glitch, borrowing the technology from pulsar astrophysics, where sudden changes in spin rate are also of interest (*Science News*, May 19, 1973, p. 321).

> Spinning off wisps can make a pulsar glitchy (*New Scientist*, August 26, 1971, p. 452).

Yiddish loans after the 1950s included more verbs and adjectives than ever before, the latter especially with numerous variants reflecting Yiddish gender distinctions: *goyish* 'non-Jewish' (neuter), *goyishe* (feminine), *goyisher* (masculine):

> I even know some Jewesses . . . whose hair is so miserably straight and *goyish* that they cry in their pillows (Milton Mayer, *Harper's*, July 1965, p. 44).

> A nice Jewish boy . . . playing desperately at being a Goyisher snob (Michael McNay, *Manchester Guardian Weekly*, September 26, 1970, p. 21).

> I'm sure that when with that blithe goyische brass . . . you approached me for a "word or two by way of preface," you were bargaining for a benediction, not a curse (John Updike, *Bech: A Book*, 1970, p. vii).

Similarly the word *meshuge* 'crazy' (used only predicatively in both Yiddish and English) was joined by the attributive adjective *meshugene* and the noun *meshugas* 'craze':

> "He [Hugh Hefner] sits around that *meshuganah* mansion all day writing about the sex life of a guppy" (Don Rickles, *Time*, October 18, 1968, p. 42).

The secretary shrugged. "Everybody's got his own *mishogas*," she said (Calvin Trillin, *Atlantic*, January 1968, p. 43).

Yiddish idioms, transferred in unanalyzed form into English, also became frequent after the 1950s. To many old Yiddish idioms that have survived to this day, e.g., *mame loshn* 'Yiddish' (lit., 'mother tongue'), *goldene medine* 'America' (lit., 'golden country'), and *yidishe mame* 'Jewish mother,' others were added. For example, *halvay* 'would that (it be so),' *gotenyu* 'dear God,' *a shande un a kharpe* 'a shame and disgrace':

> If only he could have lived out his days as ignorant of 39 Whitehall Street and its parade of humans, like livestock at a show—*halvai*! (Herbert Tarr, *The Conversion of Chaplain Cohen*, 1963, Avon ed., p. 14).

> He lived in pain, pain his only memory, questioning the necessity of it, inveighing against it, also though with affection, against God. Why *so much*, Gottenyu? (Bernard Malamud, *The Magic Barrel*, 1958, Pocket Book ed., p. 51).

> I was appointed groundskeeper and sexton of the prison church (the Jewish inmates . . . were aghast; "*A shonda und a charpah!*") (Ralph Ginzburg, *New York Times Magazine*, December 3, 1972, p. 146).

Morphological adaptation was also going on apace. Plurals took on English forms (*goys* instead of *goyim*, *shtetls* instead of *shtetlekh*), verbs acquired English inflections (*platsed* 'burst,' *shtuping* 'pushing,'), and various Yiddish loanwords were clipped, extended through derivation, or altered in function. Thus the word *nebbish* [or better, *nebish*] took on the functions of an interjection, adjective, and noun, while its etymon, Western Yiddish *nebish*, functioned only as an interjection meaning 'a pity' (so also the corresponding Eastern Yiddish *nebekh*):

interjection: Whatever they do, he'll say:
                                 Nebich! It's a pity! (Henry
                                 Roth, *Atlantic*, July 1969, p.
                                 60).

adjective: The central character is so
                                 nebbish he has not even a
                                 name (London *Times*, April
                                 6, 1968, p. 21).

noun: He starts as a bandy-legged
                                 nebbish: jumpy, up tight, the
                                 least-likely-to-succeed mob-
                                 ster you have ever seen (Dan
                                 Sullivan, *New York Times*,
                                 August 8, 1968, p. 28).

In turn the noun was shortened to *neb*:

Sasha retaliates with cuckoldry—but, considering what a *neb*
he is, her infidelity does not even the feminist score (Marilyn
Bender, *New York Times*, April 23, 1972, p. 36).

Derivations have yielded some peculiar English forms. One
writer, on the analogy of *goyisher, yidisher, heymisher,* etc.
derives an adjectival form *nebbisher* from the noun *nebbish*:

In an eerie, Brooklyn fashion, Max is a *nebbisher* Lear . . .
(Brendan Gill, *New Yorker*, December 12, 1968, p. 180).

And from *meshuge* 'crazy' an American Jewish writer derives
the form *meshuganess* (perhaps by confusion with *meshugas*):

You should come here because you'll find a wider degree of
neuroses, mental imbalance and narishkeit (meshuganess) than
you'll find in the country (Israel Shenker, *New York Times*,
September 27, 1968, p. 45).

(*Narishkayt* is a Yiddish loan meaning 'folly.') The more common type of derivative is on the order of *schlocky* 'inferior, junky,' *schlockiness; klutzy* 'clumsy,' *klutziness, klutzily*; *knishery* 'place where knishes are sold,' and the like. The influence on American English of two Yiddish morphological forms, namely the prefix *shm-* (in hundreds of reduplications like *value-shmalue, Oscar-Shmoskar, revolution-shmevolution*) and the agent suffix *-nik*, is so well known that a discussion of these morphemes seems almost superfluous. The deprecatory prefix *shm-*, which has been subjected to thorough analysis elsewhere,[31] is still commonly used, as in the following:

[He] admonished the chorus, saying, "Text, schmext, just keep it peppy. And don't fidget during the solos" (*New Yorker*, November 7, 1977, p. 49).

Shm- is often used with a jocular follow-up clause, as in "Oedipus, shmoedipus—as long as he loves his mother" or "Cancer, shmancer—as long as you're healthy."

As for the suffix *-nik*, its popularity in American English did not arise directly from Yiddish but rather from the currency in the late 1950s of *sputnik* (1957) and especially of its immediate offspring, *beatnik* (1958). It should be stressed at the same time that the familiarity of Americans with such Yiddishisms as *allrightnik, no-goodnik, holdupnik,* and *nudnik* contributed greatly to the immediate and wide acceptance of the suffix *-nik* once *sputnik* made its debut. So it is erroneous to ascribe the spread of the *-nik* suffix in American English wholly to *sputnik* and *beatnik*. In this connection, the notion that *no-goodnik* was an American English coinage (*no good* + *-nik*) is also probably mistaken. In all likelihood it was an American Yiddish word formed by blending English *no good* with the near-homophonous Russian word *negódnik*, meaning 'a good-for-nothing,' exactly what *no-goodnik* means. (The Russian word is a derivative of the adjective *negódnyi* 'bad, unworthy, unsuitable,' itself a compound of *ne* 'not, no' + *gódnyi* 'fit, proper, good.') It is not surprising that Russian Jewish immigrants using *negódnik* in the United States were thought by their American relatives to be saying *no-goodnik*, as both the forms and meanings of the base words were nearly identical in the immigrants' pronunciation.

The best known American English *-nik* word borrowed from Yiddish has been the informal and often humorous *nudnik* 'a bore, pest, nag,' which Yiddish took or formed from a Slavic (probably Polish) word.[32] The earliest citation for the term in the OED Supplement (Vol. II, 1976) is dated 1947.[33] The following are examples from the fifties and sixties:

> "No one knew me," recalls Zarchin. He was referred to as a "*nudnik*" (pedantic fusspot) (*Time*, September 3, 1956, p. 48).

> I like to go down to Delancey Street for a nosh and kibitz with the nudnicks in Yonah Schimmel's (Ronald Sukenick, quoted in *Saturday Review*, July 6, 1968, p. 26).

From a related Yiddish word, the verb *nudyen* 'to bore, pester,' American English obtained the verb (soon changed in function to a noun) variously spelled *nudzh, noodge*, or, by influence of the English word of the same spelling, *nudge*. *Nudge* (with the *u* pronounced as in *put*) was probably influenced in meaning by English *nag* and as a noun it is a synonym of *nudnik*; in any case, it should not be confused with the standard English noun *nudge*, meaning 'a slight push.'[34]

> "He's not a writer, he's a nudge. On the phone twice a day asking how's it going!" (William Cole, *New York Times Book Review*, December 3, 1972, p. 56).

> Discharged from prison, Lou Jean Poplin—sometime beautician, full-time *nudzh*—must first spring her husband

Clovis . . . from the minimum-security prison (*Time*, April 15, 1974, p. 92).

It's a soupa dialect. If you don't like it, don't be a noodge. Lean off (William Safire, *New York Times Magazine*, May 18, 1980, p. 18).

From *nudge* American English derived the informal adjective *nudgy* 'pestering, annoying':

"Being with a child a certain amount of time in a relaxed and playful way instead of being trapped all day with a nudgy, irritating child is better for both mother and child," she said (*New York Times*, March 13, 1984).

Functional change of Yiddish loanwords was not limited to slang terms. For example, the noun *bar mitzvah* took on the function of a verb (usually in the passive). Since the closest equivalent in Yiddish is *vern bar mitsve* 'to become bar mitzvah,' in which the noun remains uninflected, careful writers have long been holding out for "to become bar mitzvah." The inflected form, however, has been recorded in American English since 1947 (*Webster's Ninth Collegiate Dictionary*) and is not likely to disappear from common usage:

My father grew up in a more religious family, studied Hebrew and was bar mitzvahed when he was thirteen (E. G. Smith, *Harper's*, August 1956, p. 36).

"I'd just been bar mitzvahed when I went off with my brother to pitch snake oil on the Pennsylvania carnival circuit" (Irvin Feld, quoted in *Time*, May 4, 1970, p. 74).

Another possible extension in English of a Yiddish-origin word is *shmir*. Literally meaning 'smear,' in Yiddish slang it also means 'a bribe' (and as a verb, *shmirn* 'to bribe'). In this sense it was taken over by American English about 1961 and it is still so used, as in the following:

> Danny! This is Father Flynn. Listen, lad, they've got you surrounded. In the name of all that's holy COME DOWN and give them a schmeer! (Cartoon legend, *Harper's*, November 1974, p. 86).

However, in the mid-1960s the word began to appear in an entirely new sense in English, usually in the phrase *the whole schmear,* meaning the whole business. The phrase may have come as a part translation from Yiddish but also possibly from German, which has *die ganze Schmiere* in the same sense. Here are two illustrations of this usage:

> We never learned to sit on a horse; we missed out on the whole chivalry *schmear* (Gilbert Rogin, *New Yorker,* December 18, 1971, p. 33).

> His own quest took him through the whole schmear and he lived to see the Holy Grail turn into a booby-trapped jerry (London *Times,* February 21, 1970, p. 1).

In the sixties and seventies the advertising industry became aware of the popularity of Yiddishisms and proceeded to use them widely in advertisements, especially those aimed at the Jewish market. Feinsilver gives several examples of possible Yiddish loan translations (some may be pseudo-Yiddish) used in ads, such as "who needs it?" "That's all I need!"[35] But there are more obviously Yiddish-derived ones, such as those that use actual Yiddish loanwords. The English-language newspaper and magazines of the Jewish community constantly carry advertisements of this type:

> Sanka coffee: We got where we are on pure ta'am! (*tam* 'taste')

> Brim coffee: And when it comes to ta'am—Brim is so deliciously rich.

Sunsweet prunes: Nosh on America's No. 1 prune. (*nash* 'nibble')

Maxim coffee: My husband's a "perked coffee" mayvin. He insists on Maxim. (*meyvn* 'expert')

Gulden's mustard: The smart balabosta knows that garnish is far from gornischt. (*baleboste* 'housewife,' *gornisht* 'nothing')

Manischewitz: Try the Souper Soups. Another mychel from Manischewitz. (*maykhl* 'dish, treat')

Mica-Mart: With discounts like these you'll see why it's well worth the "schlep" to Mica-Mart!

Grape-Nuts cereal: We don't potchkeh with natural goodness. (*patshke* 'mess around')

From the sixties onward Yiddishisms also became more frequent in British publications. Though Yiddish is still spoken by many Jews in Britain, its influence on British English has not been studied and may, in fact, be inconsequential, due in part to the relative smallness of the Jewish population (about four hundred thousand, over half of which is concentrated in the Greater London area). Thus the current use of Yiddishisms in British English is probably the result of American influence or at least of the example set by American writers and speakers. The only Yiddish loanword that has become thoroughly established in British English is *nosh*.

Evening nosh depended on what was going on at special prices (Diana Childe, *Punch*, January 24, 1962, p. 191).

Nosh became widespread in Britain both as a noun and verb in the late 1950s and developed various senses which are not found either in Yiddish or American English (the latter, incidentally, has also a variant form *nash*, which is orthographically closest to the Yiddish form).

In British English the noun *nosh* may mean not just 'a snack, tidbit' (as in Yiddish and American English) but also 'a meal' or 'food' in general, as well as 'a snack bar or restaurant.' A single citation in the OED Supplement (Vol. II, 1976), from a letter dated 1917, indicates that the use of *nosh* in the sense of a snack bar or restaurant was probably the earliest. In turn the verb can mean variously to nibble on food, eat a snack, eat a meal, or eat generally. The word has also spawned derivatives that are attested both in American and British English, notably *noshery* 'a restaurant or snack bar' (compare American English *knishery* 'knish shop'), *noshable*, and *nosh-up* 'a meal.' The noun *nosher* (1957) was probably taken directly from Yiddish *nasher* rather than derived from *nosh*. The following are several other examples of Yiddishisms used in British periodicals:

> Mr. Steiger's varied *personae* include an O'Casey-quoting Oirish priest, a Yiddisher plumber, . . . and a mincing, peroxided wig-creator (Michael Billington, London *Times*, May 16, 1968, p. 15).

(Note *Yiddisher*, not "Jewish," as might have been written at one time.)

> My delicatessen punster was doing a rush business; the customers were, in a lovely combination of Liverpool and Jewish humour, buying him out 'lox, schtuck, and bagel" (Stanley Reynolds, *Manchester Guardian Weekly*, March 28, 1968, p. 9).

(The author probably meant *shtik*, not "schtuck," but in trying to approximate the spelling to English *stock*, reached out for the spelling of the related German *Stück* 'piece, bit, part.')

> Strictly between ourselves, this George Chuvalo is a punk has-been Mister Nowhere, and I talked the whole megillah over

with Cassius and he reckons you'd be a better draw (Angelo Dundee, *Punch*, March 23, 1966, p. 416).

The expression "the whole megillah" is a partial loan translation of Yiddish *di gantse megile* (lit., 'the whole scroll'), the original allusion being to the long Scroll of Esther, which is read on the holiday of Purim. Apparently the phrase surfaced in English simultaneously on both sides of the Atlantic in the 1950s. Here is a recent American example:

> She [Mrs. Jane Barbe, of Atlanta] uses expressions like "the whole megillah" (meaning the whole long story) (*New Yorker*, August 16, 1976, p. 26).

Loan translations of Yiddish idioms and other typical Yiddish modes of expression abound in American English, notably in usages intended for humorous or whimsical effect. Advertisers are especially prone to employ Yiddish-sounding turns of phrase to attract attention. For example a recent advertisement for Philadelphia brand cream cheese carried the four-word legend: "Such a cream cheese!"—a direct translation of the Yiddish interjection *Aza . . . !* expressing admiration or wonder. Or one for Brim decaffeinated coffee: "Now there's ground coffee that tastes great without caffeine. So enjoy." *Enjoy* as an intransitive verb is an American Yiddishism derived from the hortative "Enjoy, Enjoy!" The phrase formed the title of a book (1960) by Harry Golden, which may have helped popularize it. The duplicative construction is characteristic of Yiddish: go, go already, eat, eat, etc. In the following quotation the phrase is used as an adjective:

> Whenever they felt money would lose its value, people would gorge themselves. It's a dancing over the volcano attitude, an enjoy-enjoy philosophy (Marylin Bender, quoting George Kaplan in the *New York Times*, January 8, 1968, p. 120).

The inversion of word order reproducing Yiddish sentence patterns (along with the pertinent intonation) is another popular device. "*This* is responsibility?" (from a *New York Times* editorial headline) turns an English declarative form into an interrogative. Another example of this type of inversion is the last sentence in the following quote:

> Bokonon points out that God made man and man asked what was the purpose of life, and God replied, "Everything must have a purpose?" (Richard Todd, *Atlantic*, May 1973, p. 106).

In Rosten's *Hooray for Yiddish!*, a book somewhat more carefully and critically prepared than his earlier *The Joys of Yiddish*, many of the entries are devoted to Yiddish intonational patterns that have been transferred to English. Some examples are: Affirming indignation by repeating a question in the form in which it was asked, with varying intonational emphasis; agreement as a vehicle of scorn; anger via sardonic exoneration, deploying "only," "merely," or 'just" to convert the factual into the embarrassing (e.g., "Don't apologize, dear: you're merely twenty-eight minutes late"); aspersion (ridicule, irony) through apparently innocent interrogation; echoing a question to maximize indignation (without stressing so much as a syllable); scorn achieved by placing the grammatical object before the grammatical subject (e.g., "*Thanks* she expects for losing my credit cards?"). This is an area of Yiddish influence that needs much more attention than it has been accorded so far.

Rosten also lists well-known colloquial usages that are possibly (and often undoubtedly) translations of Yiddish constructions. Some of these have also been cited by Feinsilver, Gold, and others:

> Again with . . . (*Shoyn vider mit . . .*)

> Better you (he, etc.) should . . . (*Beser zolst du, zol er,* etc.)

Be well (*Zay gezunt*)

Don't ask (*Freg nit* or *nisht*)

Enough already (*Genug shoyn*)

Do me (him, etc.) something (*Tu mir epes*)

Enough with . . . (*Genug mit . . .*)

Go know (*Gey veys*)

Idiomatic or proverbial expressions have been allotted less space in books dealing with the Yiddish influence on English than they deserve. Among the few Rosten includes in his latest book is the expression *every Monday and Thursday*, as used in the following quotation:

> Every Monday and Thursday the Arabs raise the price of oil, and each time they do we have to run a little faster to remain in the same place (*New York Times*, March 22, 1979, p. A22).

Every Monday and Thursday is a translation of the Yiddish idiom *yedn montik un donershtik*, meaning 'regularly, constantly, too often' in allusion either to the fact that a portion of the Torah is read and extra prayers are recited in the synagogue each Monday and Thursday or to the ancient custom of devout Jews to fast every Monday and Thursday.

A letter writer recently wrote the American columnist Ann Landers that if people would return the junk mail they receive the senders would stop sending it to them. To this suggestion Landers replied:

> Dear Fred: From your mouth to God's ears. (*New York Daily News*, July 2, 1980, p. 61).

The expression used by the columnist, who hails from a Yiddish-speaking background, is a translation of the Yiddish phrase *fun dayn moyl in gots oyrn.*

Another proverbial expression, cited in *The Taste of Yiddish,* is "It's the kind of job that just can't be done 'on one foot.' "[36] The Yiddish idiom *oyf eyn fus* 'on one foot' is itself a translation of a Hebrew-derived idiom in Yiddish, *bregel akhas* or (literally) *al regel akhas.* The expression is based on a famous Talmudic story (*Shabbat* 31a) in which a Gentile asked the scholar Hillel to teach him the entire Torah while he, the Gentile, stood on one foot. To which the sage agreed by summing up the teachings of Judaism in one sentence: "What is hateful to thee, do not unto another."

To break one's head, meaning 'rack one's brains' is another recent idiom in American English. According to David Gold, it is a translation of Yiddish *brekhn zikh dem* (or *di*) *kop* (lit., 'to break oneself the head'), which has recently also entered Modern Hebrew (*shavar et harosh,* lit., 'to break the head').[37]

A phrase that became established in American English during the 1970s is *the bottom line,* meaning 'the net result, upshot, conclusion.' The phrase is a literal translation of the Yiddish idiom *di untershte shure,* and its figurative meaning is identical with that of the Yiddish phrase. In Yiddish usage, a speaker may proceed to sum up a lengthy discourse with the sentence, *Di untershte shure iz . . . ,* or an impatient listener may demand, *Vos iz di untershte shure?* 'What is the bottom line?' The original reference may have been to the concluding line or "punch line" of a story, the final figure on a balance sheet, or the line registering the sum total of any calculation. The earliest citations in English suggest that the phrase first surfaced in financial and commercial circles in New York, where one frequently hears accountants, stockbrokers, salesmen, and merchants use Yiddish words and expressions. According to the writer Tuvia Preschel (writing in the Hebrew weekly *Hadoar*), the Yiddish phrase has also been taken into

Modern Hebrew as *hashura haakhrona*. The following quotations illustrate the use of this phrase during the early seventies:

> With all those mergers, and today's emphasis on the bottom line, knowing the right way to fire is an indispensable management skill (Advertisement for *Fortune* magazine in *Advertising Age*, quoted in *New Yorker*, November 11, 1972, p. 191).

> And the bottom line of the lesson is simple: Throw away your analysts, your figures, and your chart board (Cleveland Amory, *Saturday Review*, December 18, 1973, p. 13).

> . . . a complicated explanation, the bottom line of which is that money is small (Melvin Durslag, *TV Guide*, July 13, 1974, p. 15).

It seems appropriate to close this chapter by asking what is "the bottom line" with respect to the influence of Yiddish on English. That the influence has been considerable and even remarkable is self-evident. The proof lies in the fact that the Yiddish loans listed by Mencken over fifty years ago are still firmly entrenched in American English informal and slang usage. Surely the influence of Yiddish on American English was deemed significant when in 1980 J. L. Dillard, in *Perspectives on American English*, reprinted over fifty pages from Feinsilver's *The Taste of Yiddish*, that extract making up the longest paper in the collection.[38] The question to ask now is whether this influence will continue or wane, whether it will grow or decline and possibly even disappear in the foreseeable future. The answer to that depends essentially on what the bilinguals in the American Jewish population will do in the future. They are the ones who maintain the reservoirs of Yiddish from which they draw the loanwords and loan translations that eventually make their way into the mainstream of American English. The time has come now to talk about the variety of English used by this group of speakers.

Jewish English in
the United States

6

The idea of a Jewish variety or dialect of English (whether of New York English, American English, British English, etc.) is not new. As far back as 1928, H. B. Wells referred to a successor to American Yiddish, which he called "Judeo-English," when he wrote, "There is no reasonable doubt that American Yiddish will within a very few years lose its identity, at least as Judeo-German, will turn into Judeo-English, expire quietly, and finally become as delightfully musty and passé a subject for doctor's theses as Anglo-Saxon is today."[1] Professor Wells' delightfully musty prediction of the fate of Yiddish did not come true "within a very few years," nor has it come true well over fifty years after his Cassandra-like prophecy; but no matter. He did dimly foresee the development of a "Judeo-English," by which he meant a Jewish form of English which would replace the Jewish form of German ("Judeo-German") which he conceived Yiddish to be.

Soon afterwards, in 1932, C. K. Thomas described in an article entitled "Jewish Dialect and New York Dialect" what "might be called a clearly defined dialect which was characteristic of New York Jews."[2] Thomas' study was concerned with the speech of the first native-born generation of New York Jews, not their immigrant parents whose "Jewish accent" had long been the object of parody in popular works of humor such as Milt Gross' *Nize Baby* (1926) and Leo Rosten's *The Education of H*y*m*a*n K*a*p*l*a*n* (1937). The conclusions reached by Thomas, admittedly tentative, were that first-generation native New York Jews dentalized the alveolar consonants [t, d, n, l, s, z], i.e., they formed these sounds between the tongue and teeth instead of between the tongue and gum ridge, overaspirated the [t] sound, had difficulties with [s], and substituted [ng] for [ŋ], making *singer* rhyme with *finger*. These conclusions were initially met with skepticism and then went ignored for lack of interest in the subject.

About thirty years later, the concept of a Jewish dialect of American English was revived with the publication in 1966 of Labov's pioneering sociolinguistic work, *The Social Stratification of English in New York City.*[3] Through various ingenious techniques, Labov demonstrated that certain features of New York speech, such as a raised [o] in words like *off, cough, soft,* are more common among Jewish Americans than among Italian Americans and Irish Americans. Elsewhere Labov showed that second-generation Italian Americans patterned certain features of speech on those of Jewish Americans, who had themselves absorbed those features from the Yiddish of their forebears.[4] Labov's findings drew support from studies, such as that of George Jochnowitz, of the speech patterns of native-born children of Yiddish speakers.[5]

The ethnic revival of the late 1960s sparked a widespread interest in various ethnic varieties or dialects of English, notably Black English, Puerto Rican English, and Chicano English. While the same revival heralded a renewed interest in the Yiddish language, especially among third-generation descendants of Jewish immigrants, concern with the English of American Jews as an ethnic variety of the language dwindled and practically disappeared. It is not hard to understand why. The same powerful socioeconomic forces within the American Black, Puerto Rican, and Chicano communities that raised the ethnic consciousness of these groups, also gave impetus to the study of their respective cultures and the particular languages and dialects that embodied their cultures. Among American Jews of East European descent such a culture and language was readily available in Yiddish, which many young American Jews felt had been abandoned and forgotten by their second-generation parents. Yiddish *was* their "native" tongue, not English or any form of English, and many young Jews reached even further back in their heritage and seized upon the ancestral Hebrew as *their* language. The concept of a Jewish variety of English was thus quietly dropped, if indeed it was ever consciously picked up by linguists or Judaica scholars.

Not until the mid-1970s were some voices raised on behalf of this neglected area of study. In a 1975 review which appeared in the journal *Language,* Joshua A. Fishman called for studies of "Chicano English (e.g., Los Angeles) or Jewish English (in Flatbush, Brooklyn) or other urban varieties of English that have lived on long beyond their immigrant originators."[6] Since then, David L. Gold, of the University of Haifa, as co-editor (with Leonard Prager) of the *Jewish Language Review,* an annual published since 1981, and as a regular contributor to *Comments on Etymology,* a fortnightly journal edited by Gerald L. Cohen at the University of Missouri, has been in the forefront of the study of Jewish English, especially *"Eastern Ashkenazic English,* i.e., the variety of English whose immediate substratum is Eastern Yiddish (for at least eighty years this has been the majority variety of Jewish English)."[7]

The very concept of *Jewish English* raises a number of questions. Is it a Jewish language, in the same sense that Tsarfatic ("Judeo-French"), Italkic ("Judeo-Italian"), and Yavanic ("Judeo-Greek") were Jewish languages? In 1972, reviewing a book by Raphael Patai that dealt in some detail with Jewish languages, Richard N. Levy wrote: "From his [Patai's] description of Jewish languages, for example Yiddish, Ladino, Judeo-Arabic, et al. one can make a case for the barely perceptible beginnings of a Judeo-English—cf. words life 'halakhic,' 'tachlitic,' 'Bar Mitzvahed,' 'brissed,' etc."[8] Fishman has since put it more strongly:

> Indeed, the ultimate Jewish sociolinguistic reality today is the fact that English or some Jewish variant thereof is probably the most widespread JL [Jewish language] of our time. Whether it will succeed in becoming even more so—even in the ultra-Orthodox circles that stand to the right of Yeshiva University—should be a major topic on the agenda of all who are interested in the sociology of JLs [Jewish languages]. Is it possible that a JL is being born before our very eyes but that few are aware of it?[9]

In the same article, Fishman grapples with the problem of defining the term *Jewish language*. If it is defined, for example, on an attitudinal basis, i.e., a Jewish language is Jewish because Jews or non-Jews believe it to be Jewish, then Jewish English does not pass muster as a Jewish language, since so far it has not been recognized as such by its users or non-users. If, on the other hand, a language is defined as Jewish either because it is used in conjunction with identifiably Jewish pursuits or because it is structurally (phonologically, lexico-semantically, morpho-syntactically, etc.) different in some way from the language of coterritorial or neighboring non-Jews, then Jewish English could certainly be a Jewish language, since it qualifies on both scores.

Yet other questions remain. Who precisely are the users of Jewish English? How many subvarieties are there? What are its spatial or geographical boundary lines? Why is it not written in Hebrew characters, as Yiddish and Judezmo were even in their earliest stages? (As it happens, this last question is the easiest to answer: not all Jewish languages on record used the Hebrew alphabet, and what is more, not everything that was written in Hebrew characters was necessarily a Jewish language.)[10] Why is there a need for Jewish English, especially if

Yiddish is maintained and the use of Modern Hebrew is increasing in various segments of the American Jewish Community? Can all three coexist within the limited confines of one religio-cultural group? And just how do these three Jewish languages interrelate or affect each other? These are some of the questions raised, and most of them are at present only partially or subjectively answerable. As Fishman puts it:

> The whole notion of Judeo-English (mockingly: Yinglish, less archaically: Jewish English) still seems strange to most current investigators. Although various lexical, grammatical, prosodic and functional characteristics of JE have already been described, the major Israeli vs. American sub-varieties still remain largely uncaptured. . . . JE in the USA, as used in Yeshiva circles (and as is gaining currency in other circles with which the latter intersect), has incorporated numerous word-by-word translation calques of Yiddish paraphrastic constructions common both in learned and in popular discourse: e.g., *zay mikh mekhavn—be me mekhavn,* 'Should I be you *mekhavn?*' These are expressions learned by students from their talmud instructors. The students now study talmud in English translation. The instructors still studied it in Yiddish translation. The instructors seem to be transposing their fully routinized Yiddish translation into their English translation. The students accept this as an appropriate style of English for talmud study. Jewish languages have been born this way in the past. Under what circumstances could it happen again?[11]

It might be thought, in answer to this last question, that the circumstances for the creation of a new Jewish language in America are highly unfavorable. The freedom, mobility, and ease of acculturation enjoyed by Jews in this country would seem to preclude completely the need or desire of this group to diverge linguistically from the standard English norm. It would seem that a divergence from the norm would require a confluence of specific social, political, economic, and even geographic conditions—conditions such as enforced or voluntary isolation, religious intolerance or persecution, economic deprivation, and the like—all presently nonexistent and potentially very improbable in America. The history of Jewish languages of the past, however, denies these assumptions. The fact is that "persecution or ghettos or religious piety alone cannot maintain or create a [Jewish] language of one's own."[12] The very opposite may be true, at least in many cases; that is, for a Jewish language to thrive, the Jewish community must enjoy prolonged periods of stability, peace, and friendly relations with the Gentile community. An obvious sociological parallel to this phenomenon is the tremendous intensification of traditionalism and religious commitment among Hasidic and ultra-Orthodox Jews in the midst of the freest and most liberal environment in the world—New York City.

Another argument, advanced by modern scholars, is that the genesis of a Jewish language requires an overpowering need by the Jewish community to preserve religious and cultural differences, and it is this need that fosters and finally preserves differences in language. This is certainly a valid assumption, and one that explains the great need felt by many Jews to preserve Yiddish even in the American milieu. But does it account for the need of another Jewish language? Fishman raises the question: "If the tradition is so all-embracing and overpowering, then why was Ancient Hebrew replaced by Aramaic/Aramic in the Holy Land itself and why was Aramaic/Aramic replaced by Judeo-Greek/Yavanic and why did a whole succession of JLs subsequently arise in highly traditional immigrant/refugee communities that were obviously already speaking a JL, who were already praying in LK [*loshn koydesh*, the holy tongue, Hebrew] and who already had an LK reading/writing elite?"[13]

The answer may be supplied by the condition of Yiddish itself in this country. As an immigrant language, no matter how traditional to many Jews or how actually sacred to a minority of Jews, Yiddish has been bearing for a long time the taint of inferiority and *zhargon* that stigmatized it from the moment it arrived in this country. The current blossoming of nostalgic and ethnic interest in it has not changed the fact that it is for most American Ashkenazic Jews a second or secondary language. Is it not conceivable that Jewish English has been generated as an acceptable alternative to Yiddish, and that the same circumstances that brought about this change could have been at work when ancient Aramaic was replaced by Yavanic and when any Jewish language was replaced by another Jewish language in highly traditional immigrant colonies of the past? In short, it is not "unchanging" tradition that has changed when an old Jewish language is replaced by a new one (after all, the ancient Hebrew component always remains, by definition); what has changed is the attitude of the speakers toward the old Jewish language, which, having lost some of its prestige under new conditions and circumstances, must now be replaced by a more acceptable language that would serve henceforth as the vehicle of traditional Jewish concepts and values.

In what follows I shall attempt to give an overview (with some specifics) of an ethnocentric or traditionalist group within the American Jewish community that has developed over the past fifty years a form of Jewish English that is essentially a religion-centered variant of American Ashkenazic English, i.e., the English of American Jews of Ashkenazic origin or descent.[14] The group forms a part of the Orthodox Jewish community, in which it presently constitutes a majority. There are in the United States probably about half a million Orthodox Jews, most of whom have become "Modern" during the past half century, so that in their outward appearance they are scarcely distinguishable from their non-Orthodox coreligionists.[15] Nevertheless, Modern Orthodox Jews are strict observers of the Sabbath and the Jewish holidays, maintain their own religious day schools and yeshivas, partake only of rabbinically supervised kosher food, attend synagogues with separate seating for men and women, cover their heads with hats or skullcaps at home and in public, and generally strive to adhere to all the minutiae of rabbinic law. Thus, their highly religion-oriented private and social life acts as an effective barrier against the "assimilation" that is anathema to Orthodoxy.

There are Orthodox Jews in all major cities across the country, but the center of American Orthodoxy is, as it has always been, New York City and its environs. As there are various ideological subdivisions within Orthodoxy—from the so-called Modern Orthodox to the ultra-Orthodox and the sectarian or Hasidic—the group does not constitute a truly organized community. What sets the Orthodox apart from other Jews is their strict adherence to Jewish law and tradition. This commitment to traditional Judaism extends to all areas of life, including language.

Whereas the ultra-Orthodox and Hasidic Jews have retained Yiddish as their primary language, using it at home, in their schools, and in most of their activities, the Modern Orthodox have become by and large English speakers, though many of them are in varying degrees Yiddish-English bilinguals. But while English is their primary language, and often the only language they use (especially if they are American born), their form of English is to a greater or lesser degree influenced by, and often heavily dependent on, forms and expressions of Eastern Yiddish origin. In addition, since the establishment of the State of Israel, their Ashkenazic English has been increasingly influenced by Modern Hebrew Sephardic usages.

The particular form of American Ashkenazic English used by this group has so far received no noticeable recognition among the Modern Orthodox, not even as an extension or replacement of American Yiddish. But just as the ultra-Orthodox and the Hasidim value Yiddish only as a means of studying and expressing traditional concepts, and not as a language (though there have been occasional homages from their quarters to Yiddish qua language), so the Modern Orthodox view their own speech habits only as a natural way of expressing Jewish values and concepts, as merely another expression of *yidishkayt*. Their language is thus an insider's language. The individual who does not understand or communicate in it is spotted or treated as an outsider, and this fact exerts a certain amount of pressure on members of the group to use Jewish English as the normal medium of intragroup communication. In Modern Orthodox day schools and yeshivas the use of Jewish English is actively encouraged, as for example in the following statement by an Orthodox educator: "Although students should know how to refer to these items in English, the norm should be *Motzaei Shabbos*—not Saturday night, *daven*—not pray, *bentsch*—not recite Grace After Meals, *Yom Tov*—not holiday."[16]

Because of the emphasis on religious education among the Modern Orthodox, their educational institutions (ranging from nursery schools all the way to theological seminaries) are focal points in the perpetuation and dissemination of Jewish English. Yeshiva faculties consist in the main of bilinguals who regularly intersperse Yiddish- and Hebrew-origin words and expressions in their English, which are then adapted and internalized by their pupils and reinforced by repetition. On the whole, however, yeshiva talk is a somewhat specialized form of Orthodox Ashkenazic English, as it contains many elements of an academic and scholarly nature which do not frequently appear in the more homely speech of average Modern Orthodox men and women.

More representative of common usage is the type of Jewish English printed in the English-language periodicals of the American Orthodox community. There are over a dozen such publications on the national level, some of the best-known ones being *Jewish Life* (established 1946), *Jewish Press* (1950), *Jewish Parent* (1948), *Jewish Action* (1950), *Young*

Israel Viewpoint (1952), *Olomeinu-Our World* (1945), *Jewish Observer* (1963), *Yavneh Review* (1963), and *Tradition* (1958). In allowing a certain amount of uninhibited use of Jewish English in their pages, these periodicals not only reflect the normal speech habits of their writers and readers, but also indirectly endow this form of speech with prestige, reinforcing its use among the initiated, educating uninitiated readers in it, and setting up standards and conventions of Jewish-English usage.

The following excerpts from several of these so-called Anglo-Jewish periodicals are representative of the American Ashkenazic form of Jewish English used by the Modern Orthodox:

> Tisha B'Av 5733 it was finally by zechus to be in Eretz Yisroel. I thought I would be able to daven at the Kosel. . . . Our madrichim, however, felt otherwise (*Jewish Observer,* November 1973, p. 28).

(*Tisha B'Av* 'Ninth of Av,' a fast day [transliterated from Hebrew; pronounced *tishebov*]; 5733, a year of the Jewish calendar; *zechus* 'privilege resulting from accumulated merits' [properly spelled *zkhus*]; *Eretz Yisroel* 'Land of Israel' [properly *Erets*]; *daven* 'say the prescribed prayers'; *Kosel* 'Western Wall' [Ashkenazic Hebrew reflex of Modern Hebrew *kotel*, lit., 'wall']; *madrichim* 'leaders' [properly *madrikhim,* plural of *madrikh*])

> The yeshiva bocherim are dancing, . . . it is time to b'dek the kallah. Hush, the chossen, Aaron Shlomo approaches. . . . He is her besherte, her chosen one (*Jewish Press,* October 31, 1975, p. 13).

(*yeshiva bocherim* 'yeshiva students' [properly spelled *bokherim,* plural of *bokher,* lit., 'youth']; *b'dek the kallah* 'place a veil over the bride,' a Jewish wedding custom [from

Yiddish *badekn di kale*, lit., 'cover the bride']; *chossen* 'bridegroom' [properly *khosn*]; *besherte* [properly *basherte*, feminine of *basherter* 'predestined one,' erroneously used in the citation as a masculine due to blurring of gender distinctions by English influence])

> Whatever the reason one wants to be with a Boro Park family—for a simcha, for a shidduch, for companionship, for chinuch, for chizuck, . . . the Committee and its 90 baalei battim welcome you (*Jewish Journal*, December 12, 1975, p. 22).

(*simcha* 'happy occasion, celebration' [properly spelled *simkhe*]; *shidduch* 'marital match' [properly *shidekh* or, in Ashkenazic Hebrew, *shidukh*]; *chinuch* 'Jewish education' [properly *khinekh* or, in Ashkenazic Hebrew, *khinukh*]; *chizuck* 'strengthening (of faith)' [properly *khizek* or, in Ashkenazic Hebrew, *khizuk*]; *baalei batim* 'members of a congregation or community' [properly *balebatim*])

> Mr. Luxemberg . . . delivered the Dvar Torah at the Shabbat afternoon seudah (*Young Israel Viewpoint*, March 1976, p. 11).

(*Dvar Torah* 'Torah discourse' [from Yiddish *dvar toyre*, lit., 'word of Torah']; *Shabbat* 'Sabbath' [from Modern Hebrew *shabat*]; *seudah* 'festive meal')

> We have in our city of about 100,000 Yidden, ken yirbu, four great modern orthodox shools. . . . Each caters to Barmitzvahs on Shabboth, with all the chillul shabboth befarhessia involved (*Jewish Life*, May 1966, p. 60).

(*Yidden* 'Jews' [*yidn*, plural of *yid* 'Jew']; *ken* [or *keyn*] *yirbu* 'may they multiply,' lit., 'thus they shall increase'; *shool* 'synagogue' [misspelling of standard Ashkenazic English *shul*]; *Shabboth* 'Sabbath' [properly *shabes* or, in Ashkenazic

Hebrew, *shabos*]; *chillul shabboth befarhessia* 'public dese-
cration of the Sabbath' [properly *khilel shabes bifresye* or, in
Ashkenazic Hebrew, *khilul shabos biferhesye*])

> In some shuls the gabbai carries around three pushkas (*Kol
> Yavneh,* September–October 1974, p. 19).

(*shuls* 'synagogues'; *gabbai* 'trustee, officer'; *pushkas* 'charity
boxes')

> My host bought an aliya for me, but I didn't know about it until
> the shammus, according to the minhag of the yekkis, handed
> me a silver-plated aliyah card (*Jewish Press,* July 4, 1975, p.
> 24).

(*aliyah* 'the honor of being called up to the Torah-reading desk
at the synagogue to recite the blessings over the Torah scroll'
[properly *aliye*]; *shammus* 'synagogue beadle' [properly
shames]; *minhag* 'custom'; *yekkis* 'German Jews' [often dis-
paraging]; *aliyah card* 'card indicating the section of the
Torah-reading for which the holder is called up')

> We must practice Ahavoh not Sinoh; we must build Yid-
> dishkeit, not destroy it. If a non-frum boy moves into your
> neighborhood, . . . be mekarev him (*Darkenu,* July 1975, p.
> 7).

(*Ahavoh* 'love' [for Ashkenazic Hebrew *ahavo*]; *Sinoh*
'hatred, hate' [for Ashkenazic Hebrew *sino*]; *Yiddishkeit*
'Judaism' [properly *yidishkayt*]; *non-frum* 'nonreligious'; *be
mekarev* 'draw near, befriend')

> The Gaon in Torah, Reb Chaim Zimmerman, *shlita,* . . .
> drove home the point again and again that, "You don't pasken
> a sha'alah with drush" (*Jewish Life,* July 1973, p. 13).

(*Gaon* 'great scholar' [transliterated from Hebrew; pronounced *goen*]; *Reb* 'respectful form of address for a man'; *shlita* 'may he live long and happily' [an acronym]; *pasken* 'make a ruling on a legal question' [properly *paskn*]; *sha'alah* 'a question on a point of law' [transliterated from Hebrew; pronounced *shayle*]; *drush* 'homiletic [aggadic] interpretation')

> How about articles on midos, chesed, musar, Taharas Hamishpachah . . . shidduchim . . . Kupat Cholim . . . Aishes Chayils (*The Jewish Woman's Outlook*, January 1983, p. 10).

(*midos* 'moral and ethical values' [Ashkenazic Hebrew form; Yiddish *mides*]; *chesed* 'mercy, favor, helping others' [properly spelled *khesed*]; *Taharas Hamishpachah* 'observance of the laws of family purity' [properly *tahares hamishpokhe*]; *shidduchim* 'matchmaking' [properly *shidukhim*]; *Kupat Cholim* 'medical insurance fund' [from Modern Hebrew]; *Aishes Chayils* 'women of valor' [properly *eyshes khayils*])

Though the above passages are written in English, their syntax frequently reflects Yiddish syntactic patterns, as though they were translations from Yiddish, though the writers were obviously not consciously translating as they wrote. Many of the English words and phrases can be analyzed as loan translations of Yiddish equivalents: hush (*sha*), bought an aliyah (*gekoyft an aliye*), carries around (*trogt arum*), etc. Yiddish is thus reincarnated in English form, and the Ashkenazic English of the Modern Orthodox, while English in structure, is built on an infrastructure of American Yiddish with a smattering of Modern Hebrew elements. Also noteworthy is the fact that the burden of meaning of each of these excerpts is carried by the Yiddish loanwords; the English words serve only as the structural or grammatical vehicle for conveying the meaning expressed by the loanwords.

As the citations show, the Ashkenazic English of the Modern Orthodox (henceforth Orthodox Ashkenazic English) is used to express the elements that characterize traditional Jewish life: rituals and customs, family and personal conduct, the educational and intellectual sphere, the historical and cultural sphere. Thousands of words and expressions have been borrowed from Yiddish and Hebrew to designate the host of things and activities that pertain to Jewish living, especially words with emotional overtones (negative and positive). The borrowings include, for example, terms pertaining to marriage: *shidekh* or *shidukh* 'marital match,' *shadkhn* 'matchmaker,' *be meshadekh* 'make a match,' *zivig* 'destined match or mate,' *nadn* 'dowry,' *khasene* 'wedding'; terms relating to death: *levaye* 'funeral,' *hesped* 'eulogy,' *be maspid* 'eulogize,' *ovl* 'mourner,' *nifter* 'the deceased,' *matseyve* 'gravestone'; terms dealing with study: *talmid* 'student,' *talmid khokhem* 'learned person,' *melamed* 'religious teacher,' *limed* or *limud* 'learning, study,' *limudey koydesh* 'sacred studies,' *lamdn* 'Jewish scholar'—all of these Yiddish-origin words derive ultimately from the same ancient Hebrew root; terms of kinship: *zeyde* 'grandfather,' *bobe* or *bube* 'grandmother,' *tate* 'father,' *mame* 'mother,' *mekhutn* 'in-law,' *shviger* 'mother-in-law,' *eynikl* 'grandchild'; designative and descriptive terms: *balebos* 'male head of household' (feminine *baleboste*), *balebatish* 'respectable,' *freilekh* 'merry, jolly' (also *a freilekhs*, a lively tune suitable for folk dancing), *shokhn* 'neighbor,' *khaver* 'companion, friend,' *prostak* 'coarse person,' *prost* 'coarse, vulgar'; a unique class of preventive terms: *halevay* or *alevay* 'would that it be so,' *lehavdl* 'without meaning to equate, no comparison intended,' *beli neyder* 'no vow intended,' *kanehore* or *kan ayn hore* '(may) no evil eye (befall),' *kholile* 'heaven forbid'; forms of address, titles, and honorifics: *rebe* 'teacher,' also 'Hasidic leader,' *harabonis* or *rebetsn* 'rabbi's wife,' *zal* 'of blessed memory,' *olov hasholem* 'may he rest in peace'; greetings and farewells: *zay gezunt* 'be well,' *kol tuv* 'all the best,' *gut vokh* 'a good week,' *borkhabe* or *borukh habo* 'welcome'; exclamations and expletives: *gevald* 'hue and cry, alarm,' *a mekhaye* 'a delight, pleasure,' *yemakh shmoy* '(may) his name be blotted out'; monosyllabic interjections: *nu* 'well, so,' *sha* 'quiet, hush,' *na* 'here, take,' *fe* 'ugh, disgusting,' *oy* 'oh, dear'; and numerous idiomatic expressions: *a nekhtiker tog* 'nothing of the sort, lit., 'yesterday's day,' *abi gezunt* 'as long as there is health,' *bobe mayse* 'tall tale,' *drey a kop,* 'muddle one up,' lit., 'twist a head.'

Many of the Yiddish-origin nouns in Orthodox Ashkenazic English have synonyms taken from Hebrew and sometimes also equivalents formed in English. For example, *yarmlke* 'skullcap' is interchangeable with Hebrew-derived *kipa*; *yidishkayt* 'Judaism' with *yahadus* (or *yahadut*); *bekher* 'wine cup used on festive occasions' is synonymous with either *kos* or the Jewish-English compound *kidish cup* or *kidush cup*; *shvartses* 'blacks' is synonymous with *shkhoyrim*, and *gut shabes* (Sabbath greeting) with *shabbat shalom*, and so on.

The increasing influence of Modern Hebrew in Orthodox Ashkenazic English is reflected in the tendency to spell, but not necessarily to pronounce, Yiddish loanwords of Hebrew origin according to their Modern Hebrew pronunciation. Thus the familiar *shabes* 'Sabbath' is often spelled *Shabbat,* as in "a Shabbat party," "a Shabbat meal," and words like *ovl* 'mourner,' *bris* 'circumcision,' *talis* 'prayer shawl,' and *kosher* 'ritually fit' are frequently rendered as *avel, brit, talit,* and *kasher.* The Hebrew influence is reflected in the following exchange, where a child typically addresses her father with the Modern Hebrew word for daddy, *abba,* although the other Jewish-origin words she uses are clearly from Yiddish:

"Abba," she asked, "what are you doing?"
"Reading. . . ."

"For a class in shul, or for your drosha ['sermon'] this Shabbos?"
(*Jewish Parent*, June 1972, p. 15).

The plural inflection of many Yiddish nouns is -*s*, as it is in English; for example, *kishke* 'gut, stuffed derma,' plural *kishkes; kehile* 'community, congregation,' plural *kehiles*. However, a number of Yiddish nouns have other plurals, such as -*im* (originally the Hebrew masculine plural suffix) and -*lekh* (the plural form of the Yiddish diminutive suffix -*l*), and although words with these endings have entered Orthodox Ashkenazic English in unanalyzed forms, they have also been adapted into the English plural system, thus producing many variant pairs, such as *seyfers, sforim* 'sacred books,' *esrigs, esroygim* 'citrons used on the holiday of sukes,' *shiers, shiurim* 'lessons, lectures,' *shtetls, shtetlekh* 'Jewish villages in eastern Europe,' *kneidels, kneidlekh* 'dumplings.' The first of each of these pairs was formed by adding the English plural suffix -*s* to the singular forms.

Another typical adaptation of Yiddish loanwords is the replacement of Yiddish diminutives such as -*l* and -*ele* with the English diminutive -*ie* or -*y* (but often spelled -*i*). Thus Yiddish-origin *kepele* 'small head' has acquired the variant *keppy*, and common Yiddish forenames such as *Yosl* or *Yosele, Yankl* or *Yankele*, have been Anglicized to *Yosi* and *Yanky*. The English diminutive, moreover, often contaminates the sounded final -*e* in many Yiddish loanwords, producing for example *shmatty* in place of *shmate* 'rag,' *tshatshkie* instead of *tshatshke* 'trinket,' and *zeydi* and *bubi* instead of *zeyde* and *bube*:

When a grandchild says, "I love my Zeidi and Bubbie" the grandparents always beam at that chochmeh (*Jewish Press*, August 22, 1975, p. 48).

(*Zeidi* 'grandfather,' *bubbie* 'grandmother,' *chochmeh* [properly *khokhme*] 'bright action or saying')

It is also common in Orthodox Ashkenazic English to attach English suffixes to Yiddish words and Yiddish suffixes to English words. Thus from *frum* 'religious,' Orthodox Ashkenazic English derives *frumies* 'religious types,' from *yeke* or *yeki* 'German Jew' (often disparaging), the adjective *yekish* and the noun *yekishness,* and from *shlep* 'to drag,' the derivatives *shleppy, shleppily, shleppiness, shleppish.* In the reverse process, it derives *boyele* from English *boy* (compare *boytshik* and *boytshikl,* formed in American Yiddish), *checkele* 'small check' from English *check,* and *JDLnik* from *JDL* (Jewish Defense League). The suffix -*nik* is commonly used to form new words, for example *aliyanik* 'one who makes aliya' (emigrates to Israel), *Chabadnik* 'member of Chabad (a Hasidic sect),' *hesdernik* 'Israeli yeshiva student and soldier,' and *bal tshuvenik* 'Jew who has turned religious.'[17]

It should be noted, of course, that some of the words and features described above have long been similarly used by first- and second-generation American Jews outside the Modern Orthodox community, and a considerable number of them have infiltrated general American usage. But it is not clear where in the American Jewish population particular usages arose and by what mechanisms they passed into currency among non-Jews.

Adverbs and adjectives of Yiddish origin are characteristically found in Orthodox Ashkenazic English, into which they tend to be transferred in unadapted form: *avade* 'certainly,' *davke* 'purposely, precisely,' *take* 'indeed, really,' *memeyle* 'naturally,' *khaplap* 'helter-skelter,' *grob* 'thick, fat, (fig.) boorish,' *aderabe* 'on the contrary,' *gevaldik* 'extraordinary,' *Pesakhdik* 'of Passover,' *chometsdik* 'of leaven' (i.e., not for Passover use), etc. Verbs of Yiddish origin, however, receive English inflections. Thus *shnoder* 'give a donation in the synagogue' (from Yiddish *shnodern*) is conjugated *shnodered, shnoders, shnodering; mutshe* 'harass, torment' (from Yiddish *mutshn*), *mutshed, mutshes, mutshing;*

bentsh 'to pronounce a blessing' (from Yiddish *bentshn*), *bentshed, bentshes, bentshing; farbreng* 'to hold a *farbrengen* (Hasidic get-together),' *farbrenged, farbrengs, farbrenging*, as in *We were farbrenging at the rebe's tish* 'We were holding a farbrengen at the Hasidic leader's table.'

As mentioned by Fishman in a passage cited earlier in this chapter, verb forms of the type *be mekhavn* are common in yeshiva circles. These verb phrases using the auxiliary *be* are essentially loan translations of Yiddish periphrastic verbs consisting of a Hebrew invariant and the inflected auxiliary *zayn* 'to be.' For example, *be maskim* 'to agree,' *be mashpie* 'to influence,' *be moykhl* 'to forgive,' *be mevayesh* 'to humiliate,' *be mafsik* 'to interrupt prayer,' *be mekane* 'to envy.' The periphrastic conjugation is also frequent in set phrases involving ritual or custom, e.g., *be menakhem ovl* 'to pay a condolence call,' *be mevaker khoyle* 'to visit the sick,' *be maskir neshomes* 'to recite memorial prayers' (now, more commonly, *say yisker*).

Many other set phrases involving ritual have been transferred from Yiddish, especially with the verbs *make* and *say*:

make shabes 'prepare for the Sabbath' [Yiddish *makhn shabes*]

make a moytsi 'pronounce the blessing over bread' [Yiddish *makhn a moytse*]

make a lekhayim 'drink a toast' [Yiddish *makhn a lekhayim*]

make a bris 'have one's newborn son circumcised' [Yiddish *makhn a bris*]

say torah 'deliver a learned discourse' [Yiddish *zogn toyre*]

say kaddish 'recite regularly the mourner's prayer' [Yiddish *zogn kadish*] *say tilim* 'recite the Psalms (as for one who is mortally ill)' [Yiddish *zogn tilim*]

write tnoyim 'make an agreement of betrothal,' lit., write conditions [Yiddish *shraybn tnoyim*]

blow shofar 'sound the ram's horn' (as on the High Holy Days) [Yiddish *blozn shoyfer*]

sit shive 'observe the seven days of mourning after burial' [Yiddish *zitsn shive*]

fall koyrim 'prostrate oneself' (as during certain prayers, but also used figuratively) [Yiddish *faln koyrim*]

Often these and other verb phrases are not partially translated, as they are in the examples above, but rendered in full Yiddish form within English sentences. Typical examples are:

shep nakhes: *We hope you'll shep nakhes* (or *shep much nakhes*) *from the kinder.* 'We hope you'll derive (much) pride and joy from the children.'

khap shirayim: *Did you khap shirayim at the tish?* 'Did you partake of a portion of food (handed out by a Hasidic leader) at his table?'

trink a lekhayim: *Let's trink a lekhayim!* 'Let's drink a toast!'

makh a shakl: *I'm going to makh a shakl.* I'll have a drink (of liquor),' lit., 'make the blessing over liquids.'

git a geshrey: *So he gits a geshrey.* 'So he gives a holler.'

makh a tuml: *Oy, did she makh a tuml!* 'Oh, did she make a commotion!'

Compare the idiom *make a tsimes over* (someone or something) 'make a fuss over,' where only the phrase *make a tsimes*
was taken from Yiddish *makhn a tsimes (fun)*, the preposition
over being supplied by influence of English *make a fuss over*.[18]
Yiddish transfers often take on specialized meanings. For
example, the Yiddish verb *leyenen* 'to read' has reacquired in
Orthodox Ashkenazic English *to leyn* the specific meaning 'to
read publicly from the Torah (scroll)':

> Since we had only one Sefer Torah it was agreed that the
> Ashkenazim would leyn first . . . and we leyned after the roll
> call (*Jewish Life*, July 1973, pp. 45–46).

The original meaning of Yiddish *leyenen* (ultimately from Latin *legere* 'to read') was 'to read with cantillation from the
Torah,' as distinguished from Yiddish *lezn* 'to read (in general),' a word cognate with Middle High German *lesen* and Old
High German *lesan*. However, in standard Eastern Yiddish
lezn was displaced by *leyenen* as the general word for 'to
read,' though among the religious Jews *leyenen* continued to
be used both in the specific and in the general sense. It is only
in the specifically religious sense that Orthodox Ashkenazic
English adopted the word, thereby, in effect, reclaiming its
original meaning.[19]
     In yeshiva circles, the gerundial from *leyning* has, in addi-
tion to the basic meaning of 'Torah reading,' the meaning
'preparation for a Talmudic lesson,' used chiefly in the phrase
to make a leyning, i.e., to prepare the lesson ahead of the *shier*
or Talmudic lecture.
     Another example of semantic specialization is the Yiddish-
derived word *glat* 'smooth.' This adjective, having been taken
from Yiddish primarily in the phrase *glat kosher*, referring to
the flawless or "smooth" condition of a slaughtered animal's
lungs that makes the animal ritually clean by the most stringent
standards, has come to be restricted in Orthodox Ashkenazic

English to the sense of "suitable for eating according to the strictest standards" and is today widely used in such phrases as *glat meat, glat cuisine, a glat meal,* and even predicatively, as in *This meat is glat.* Similarly, Yiddish-derived *tikhl* 'woman's shawl' has become specialized as 'a shawl or kerchief worn by married Orthodox women to cover the hair,' as distinguished from a *sheytl* or woman's wig used for the same purpose (in compliance with Jewish laws of modesty).

An example of specialization of a Modern Hebrew borrowing is the word usually spelled *chai* [*khay*], literally meaning 'alive, living,' which has been adopted as a noun in the specialized sense of 'a donation of $18.' The word usually appears in the phrase *to give chai* 'to donate $18 for charity,' from the fact that the two Hebrew letters forming this word, *khet* and *yod,* are numerically equivalent to 18 (*khet* = 8; *yod* = 10), whence the idea that the number 18 symbolizes "life," an idea reinforced by the traditional concept that charity wards off death. Standard amounts of donations are *twice chai* ($36), *three times chai* ($54), and so on, *chai* being a basic unit of almsgiving. In recent years the word has been used also as the name of gold and silver pendants in the shape of this word ("chais and stars of David"). *Chai* has also been extended to mean simply '18th,' as in "to celebrate the Community Center's chai anniversary." *Bar mitzvah* [*bar mitsve*] has been similarly extended to mean '13th year' as in "Their organization has reached its bar mitzvah."

English words, in turn, have become specialized in Orthodox Ashkenazic English as a result of contact with Yiddish near-homophones. Thus, *to learn,* by influence of Yiddish *lernen* 'to study' (often applied to the study of the Torah, Talmud, and the like), is used mainly in this specific sense, as in the following example:

Students of yeshivot g'dolot . . . were able to learn in a half-day kollel, of which he was the rosh yeshiva (*Hamevaser,* November 26, 1973, p. 3).

(*yeshivot g'dolot* 'higher or advanced yeshivas' [from Modern Hebrew]; *kollel* 'yeshiva department for married men' [from Modern Hebrew *kolel*, lit., 'collective, community']; *rosh yeshiva* 'head [or dean] of a yeshiva')

By extension, the gerund *learning* is used specifically to mean 'sacred studies,' as in "he hasn't enough time for learning." The idiom *to sit and learn* is a very common expression and a direct translation of Yiddish *zitsn un lernen* 'to devote oneself full-time to sacred studies.'

Some other examples of special senses due to near-homophony are *wash* 'to wash hands ceremonially before partaking of bread' (Yiddish *vashn zikh*), as in "He already washed"; *cook* 'to boil' (Yiddish *kokhn*), as in "I cooked some potatoes"; *give* 'to take' (Yiddish *gebn*), as in "Give a look"; *by* 'with' (Yiddish *bay*), as in "The money is by him" or "They are staying by their cousins."

Orthodox Ashkenazic English is especially productive in the formation of compounds with specialized meanings. Typically such compounds consist of a Yiddish-origin noun modifying an English noun, and are often coined to fill a semantic slot created by cultural innovation. Examples of such compounds are: *matse balls* 'round dumplings made from matse meal' (*matse meal* itself is a partial translation of Yiddish *matse mel*); *sforim store* 'religious bookstore' (but compare compounds like *sforim shranks* 'bookcases for religious books,' borrowed whole from Yiddish but adapted with an English plural, the Yiddish plural being *shrenk*); *shana tova card* 'Jewish New Year card' (*shana tova* is Hebrew for 'good year'); *shabes clock* (partial translation of Yiddish *shabes zeyger*) 'automatic timer for turning on lights and appliances on the Sabbath and holidays' (since Orthodox Jews do not turn them on or off, in compliance with strict Sabbath and holiday observance); *shabes key* 'house key in the form of a tie clip or decorative pin for wearing on the Sabbath' (since carrying objects in the hands or pockets is prohibited on the Sabbath); *shabes elevator* 'elevator which automatically steps on each floor on the Sabbath' (designed for those who cannot walk up the stairs but will not desecrate the Sabbath by pushing electric buttons); and *open khupe* 'wedding ceremony performed under an open skylight or outdoors' (in accordance with Orthodox custom). The ad hoc formation of such compounds is illustrated by *sider baseball* 'school game of reading from the Jewish prayerbook' (*sider* 'Jewish prayerbook'), *ruekh band* 'Jewish folk rock group,' (*ruekh* 'soul, spirit'), *klezmer group* 'Jewish musical band' (*klezmer* 'Jewish musician'), *Pepsi cola yarmlke* 'tiny skullcap' (from its supposed resemblance to a bottle cap), *mitsvemobile* or *mitsve tank* 'van carrying Jewish religious objects to teach their use' (*mitsve* 'commandment, precept'), *khevrewoman* 'sharp or tough woman' (on the model of *khevreman*, from Yiddish), *Maccabiathon* (a Jewish sports marathon, after the Maccabiah international Jewish sports festival), *Lag B'Omerathon* (marathon held on Lag B'Omer, a Jewish festival), etc. Often compounds are proper names coined to designate products and services aimed at the Jewish market. A few examples of these suffice to illustrate the range of such names: *Ruach Revival* (a folk rock group; *ruekh* 'soul'), *Freilach orchestra* (*freilakh/freilekh* 'merry'), *Simchatone orchestra* (*simkhe* 'celebration, joy'), *Camp Kee-Tov* (Hebrew *ki tov* 'for it is good'), *Macabee bagel pizza, Mayim Chaim ginger ale* (*mayim khayim* 'spring water,' a return to the Biblical meaning, since in Yiddish the term is used to mean hard liquor), *Tam Tov cheese* (*tam tov* 'good taste'), *Chap-A-Nosh* (a restaurant; Yiddish *khap a nash*, lit., 'grab a snack'), *Dagim Fish-mish* (Hebrew *dagim* 'fish,' Yiddish *mish* 'mix'), *Renta Yenta Inc.* (an odd-jobs service, from *yente* 'busybody'), etc. So-called bilingual puns also occur frequently: *The Yentertainers* (a Yiddish-English musical comedy), *Brave Nu World* (a title of an article on science fiction by Jewish writers), *Shaun Fergusson* (supposed Irish name, from

Yiddish *shoyn fergesn* 'already forgot'), *Yenems* brand cigarette (from Yiddish *yenems* 'another's, someone else's'), and many others. Next to direct adoption from Yiddish and the forming of hybrid compounds, loan translation is the most frequent method of borrowing in Orthodox Ashkenazic English. Thus *dairy* and *meat* are translated from *milkhik* and *fleyshik*. Both sets of terms are used to describe food, dishes, and utensils involving, respectively, the use of milk and cheese products and of products made of meat or containing meat extracts—a necessary distinction, since Jewish dietary law requires complete separation of the two types of food. Hence *dairy* and *meat* are used as adjectives, as in *a dairy* (or *meat*) *meal, dairy* (or *meat*) *dishes and pots, a dairy* (or *meat*) *kitchen,* and *a dairy restaurant,* but also as nouns in this special sense, as in "This kitchen is for meat only."

Loan translations may be literal, partial, or free. Examples of literal translations from Yiddish are *the Nine Days* 'the meatless first nine days of the month of Av' [Yiddish *di nayn teg*]; *the Three Weeks* 'three weeks of public mourning before the Ninth of Av' [Yiddish *di dray vokhn*]; *the Wall* 'the Western Wall' [Hebrew *hakotel* or Yiddish *der koysl*]; and *a good week* [greeting said at conclusion of the Sabbath; Yiddish *a gut vokh*]. Partial loan translations include *candlelighting* 'ritual of lighting candles before a Sabbath or holiday, usually performed by women' [Yiddish *likhtbentshn*, lit., blessing candles]; *Purimspiel* 'Purim play,' with homophony from Yiddish *Purimshpil*; and *wear it well,* from Yiddish *trog es gezunterheyt* 'wear it in health.' Free translations, which are basically English replacements or approximations of Yiddish loanwords, are, for example, *Grand Rabbi* for *rebe* 'Hasidic leader,' *ritualarium* for *mikve* 'ritual bath,' *the Weekly Portion* for *parshe* or *sedre* 'section of the Pentateuch (assigned for a week's reading),' and *unveiling* 'dedication of a tombstone,' replacing Yiddish *matseyve shteln* 'setting up a gravestone,' from the change in the nature of the ritual developed in the United States, involving the removal of a veil from the headstone.

The use of abbreviations and acronyms, some simply romanized transfers from Yiddish or Hebrew, but some genuine innovations, occur fairly often in Orthodox Ashkenazic English writing and, to some extent, speech. Romanized Yiddish and Hebrew forms appear chiefly in the religious realm: the formula *B"H*, added to the top right-hand corner of a piece of writing (especially a letter), stands for *Beezras Hashem* 'by the help of God'; when used contextually, it could stand also for *Borukh Hashem* 'thank God.' Other forms include *I"YH* for *Im Yirtse Hashem* 'God willing' (in running speech pronounced *mirtshem*, as in *I'll see you mirtshem by the khasene* 'I'll see you, God willing, at the wedding'), *z"l* (or as an acronym, *zal*) for *zikhroyne livrokhe* 'may his (or her) memory be for a blessing,' *shats* for *shliyakh tsibur* 'cantor,' lit., 'deputy for the congregation.' An even more established convention among the Modern Orthodox is the spelling of the name of the Deity as *G-d*, also, less frequently, *A-mighty, L-rd*, etc., as a sign of reverence that derives from the ancient practice of not writing out fully (or needlessly pronouncing) any of the Divine names in other than the sacred texts.

In the secular realm, some of the facetious abbreviations cited in the previous chapter are of course established in American Ashkenazic English, and it is indeed from this source that they pass into non-Jewish varieties of American English. A few that were not mentioned because they are less generally known outside Jewish circles are *M.O.T.* "Member of the Tribe," i.e., a fellow Jew, *J.A.P.* (usually pronounced *jap*) for "Jewish American Princess," defined in Rosten's *Hooray for Yiddish!* as "an 'in' word by young American Jews to describe a rich, spoiled, or nubile Jewess," and *Ph.G.* for Yiddish *papa hot gelt* 'the father has money.'

Very few studies have been made of the pronunciation features that characterize the speech of the various groups of Jewish English speakers in this country, and none that I know of that deals specifically with the pronunciation of the Orthodox Ashkenazic Jews. I have no doubt that a phonological study of members of this group would reveal Yiddish and possibly other influences of the kind touched upon by Labov.

To sum up the main points of this chapter, there is a growing recognition among linguists that in populated urban areas where English is the chief language or one of the chief languages, the spoken and written English of the native Jewish population usually differs significantly from the English of the non-Jewish population. The aggregate of these Jewish forms of English has been labeled *Jewish English*, on the theory that this dialect or variety of English is a modern Jewish language, perhaps the most widespread Jewish language of today. In Gold's classification, the majority variety of Jewish English at present is Eastern Ashkenazic English, whose immediate substratum is Eastern Yiddish. In the United States, an American subgroup of Eastern Ashkenazic English is what I have called (American) Orthodox Ashkenazic English, named after the Modern Orthodox users of this form of Jewish English in the United States. In this chapter I have described the gross lexical, semantic, and morphological features of Orthodox Ashkenazic English, without touching upon its similarities with, and differences from, other subvarieties of Jewish English.

The Orthodox Ashkenazic English of American Jews (as distinguished, for example, from that of Israeli or of British Jews) is especially interesting in two respects: (1) It is a relatively new form of Jewish English, having come into its own after the arrival of the post-World War II wave of mainly Orthodox Jewish immigrants into the United States (numbering over 190,000), whose birth rate is today the highest of all other groups in the American Jewish community, estimated at about four children per family, as compared to the wider Jewish figure of roughly 1.8 per family.[20] (2) It is at present the only form of Jewish English with a potential for further development as a Jewish language, partly because of the inward-drawing, separatistic tendencies of the Orthodox community as the liberalizing, anti-Israel (read, anti-Jewish) pressures of the present age mount, and partly because of the constant and powerful influence of the Yiddish-speaking ultra-Orthodox and Hasidic groups, whose birth rate, incidentally, is the highest within the Orthodox camp. These two factors cannot be ignored in any study of Jewish English in the United States.

Needless to say, a definitive study of this subject has yet to be made; the present discussion is intended only as an introduction. As Rabbi Tarfon used to say, "It is not thy duty to complete the work, but neither art thou free to desist from it" (*Pirkei Avot* 2:21). I have not desisted from the work; but others will have to complete it.

Conclusion

It is time to take stock of the state of Yiddish in the United States. In retrospect, its record of survival after over a hundred years of ups and downs in this country is as much a tribute to the captivating qualities of Yiddish as it is a source of embarrassment to those who, decade after decade, have predicted its imminent demise in America. And as if mere survival amidst overwhelming cultural pressures were not enough, this minority language was able to infiltrate the English language in America to an extent unparalleled by any other foreign language transplanted here. The development of a form of Jewish English in this country based on Eastern Yiddish is a special attestation of the powerful influence of Yiddish on a large section of the American Jewish community. So on the credit side it must be said that Yiddish has scored an unusual—and certainly unforeseeable—success in this country.

However, a realistic balancing of accounts requires us also to look at the negative side of the ledger. Yiddish as a spoken language has been steadily losing ground with every passing generation, and the only areas where it is still a primary language in this country are in the relatively small ultra-Orthodox and Hasidic segment of the Jewish community and within the even smaller group comprising the loyal Yiddishists who run Yiddish culture schools, literary societies, and scholarly orga-

103

nizations in New York City and several other American and
Canadian cities. Without a new and large infusion of Yiddish-
speaking immigrants, such as those who came here in the wake
of World War II, the prospect of Yiddish surviving as a spoken
language in the next generation or two depends wholly on the
growth and development of these two groups.

There is of course a great deal of current interest in Yiddish
in the United States. More has been written in the popular
press about Yiddish since the 1970s than perhaps ever before.
Witness the following enthusiastic "state-of-the-language"
review:

> The third generation, one might say, is "returning" to the
> cultural heritage of its immigrant grandparents. And these are
> the grandchildren that are now enrolling in courses in Yiddish
> language and literature. To fulfill this need, we now have such
> Yiddish courses in Columbia University and in five colleges of
> the City University of New York. In one of these, in Queens
> College, there are now over 400 students enrolled in Yiddish
> language and literature courses, . . . and a quarterly journal,
> called "YIDDISH" has recently begun publication (1973,
> Vol. 1, No. 1) by Queens College, under the editorship of
> Professor Joseph C. Landis. And here is a partial listing of
> other colleges and universities in the United States offering
> courses in Yiddish: Brandeis University, University of
> Iowa. . . .[1]

Or the following news reports:

> In Westchester, Long Island, Manhattan, the suburbs of Con-
> necticut, Dallas, Los Angeles and many spots in between,
> Yiddish clubs and classes are springing up at community cen-
> ters, synagogues, Y's and as part of college adult-education
> programs. It is popular with retired teachers in a special pro-
> gram offered by the United Federation of Teachers.[2]

Sixty-two universities now offer courses in Yiddish and it was the need of students and scholars for texts and original source materials that led to the project's [Yiddish book collecting] creation last year.[3]

Pessimists might argue that English courses in Yiddish language and literature, proliferating even as Yiddish speech and writing are becoming obsolescent, augur anything but hope for this language. Nevertheless it might be a mistake to venture definite predictions about the fate of Yiddish in this country. Previous doomsayers have after all turned out to be quite wrong.[4] Eugene Green sounded this note of caution forty years ago:

Those who concern themselves very deeply with Yiddish culture do not care to predict the future of the language in the United States. Yet they recognize that the quesiton of its future can be raised. But who would ask and who would answer the question of whether English will survive?[5]

So it may be wisest to confine ourselves to the present tense, and for the present Yiddish is still a force to reckon with on the American cultural scene. In a way its present status is comparable to that of ancient Hebrew. Just as for two millenia Jews did not forget Hebrew even though most of them did not speak or write it (using it only for prayer and study), so Yiddish, with its large Hebrew component, retains a strong cultural hold on many of the descendants of Yiddish speakers. In the last analysis it is this emotional attachment of many Jewish Americans to the language of their forebears that has given Yiddish its long lease on American soil and that may yet extend this lease another hundred years.

Appendix I:

The Romanization of Yiddish and Yiddish-Origin Words

Yiddish, like most Jewish languages, is written in the Hebrew alphabet. But like Hebrew, it is often necessary to transcribe or transliterate Yiddish words into Roman or Latin letters so that those unfamiliar with Hebrew may be able to read the words. A systematic transcription of Yiddish has become especially necessary in recent years with the wholesale introduction of Yiddish loanwords into the English vocabulary. Yet no attempt has been made by literate users of English to avail themselves of a consistent Yiddish transcription system, though such a system, known as the YIVO system (after the YIVO Institute for Jewish Research) has been in existence for some sixty years. This system, formerly considered for adoption by the American National Standards Institute, has also been known as the American National Standard Romanization of Yiddish (or Standardized Yiddish Romanization for short).

The need of a standard romanization system for Yiddish is glaringly obvious to anyone who has ever paid the slightest attention to the way Yiddish-origin words and phrases are "transliterated" into English in most American publications. Often the same word will be spelled half a dozen different ways in various periodicals or even in a few issues of the same periodical. For example, the Yiddish-origin word for 'thief,' *ganef,* has been spelled in English variously as *gonnof, gonoph, goniff, gonef, gonof, ganof, ganav, ganov,* and *ganif.* While *ganav* is the correct romanization of the Modern Hebrew pronunciation, and *ganov* is the correct romanization of the standard Ashkenazic Hebrew pronunciation, the form *ganef* is the

106

only correct romanization of the Yiddish-origin word; all the others are impressionistic improvisations created for the nonce.

Standard English dictionaries, which perhaps more than any other institution have helped to standardize English spelling, have been conspicuously negligent in setting a standard for the spelling of Yiddish- and Hebrew-origin words. A supposed justification for the negligence is the confusion caused by Yiddish and Hebrew doublets such as *ganef/ganav, shabes/shabat, halakha/halokhe*, though a careful treatment of such terms could weed out all but the two correct forms. Yet an influential dictionary such as *Webster's Third* has no scruples about listing as many as eight different spellings for the Yiddish-origin word *shames* 'synagogue beadle': *shammash, shamash, shammas, shamas, shammes, shames, shammos*, and *shamus*, adding to boot six different spellings for the plural of this word: *shammashim, shamashim, shammasim, shamasim, shammosim* and *shamosim*. The usual explanation, that dictionary editors are not at fault, that they are merely "recording usage," falls apart in this case, since there is no "usage" to speak of where total chaos reigns. Any sensible dictionary editor would pick *one* or at most *two* spellings, preferably the ones reflecting most closely the standard Yiddish and/or Hebrew pronunciations, and "record" those as the recommended "usage." Dictionary users would forever be grateful to such an editor for establishing a norm that an educated user of English can accept and follow without vacillation.

Being myself a dictionary editor, I was under the illusion for years that standard spellings of Yiddish- and Hebrew-origin words were evolving by themselves in English through "usage." The existence of several generally accepted English spellings (however poorly transliterated or transcribed), such as *Yom Kippur, bar mitzvah* and *menorah*, persuaded me that most other frequently used Yiddishisms and Hebraisms would sooner or later be pared down to one or two standard spellings for each. It was, however, an unwarranted assumption, founded on wishful thinking. A close study of Yiddish and Hebrew loanwords in various English-language books and periodicals of recent vintage revealed such a morass of haphazard spellings, so many errors of transcription and inconsistency, such a hodgepodge and misuse of English, not to mention Yiddish and Hebrew, spelling (consider, for example, such monstrosities as *mish-*

pawchah and *mishbawcha* for the word *mishpokhe* 'family'), that I concluded that only by adopting and promoting the coherent, consistent YIVO system (and, for Hebrew, the American National Standard Romanization of Hebrew) could order be created eventually out of chaos.

And it is not hard to create order, as the (slightly modified) transcription key of the YIVO system given below (by courtesy of the YIVO Institute for Jewish Research) indicates. Perhaps the most common mistranscription that needs to be corrected is the use of German digraph *ch* to render the spirant [x] sound of Yiddish-origin words like *khutspe* 'impertinence' and *mishpokhe* 'family.' In the first place, the digraph *ch* is singularly inappropriate for English, which uses it normally to represent the sound of *ch* in *church*. Secondly, why use *ch* when the symbol *kh* is used widely to transcribe [x], as for example in Russian and Modern Greek. Yet when it comes to Yiddish, a perverse adherence to German spelling makes uncritical writers and editors use the totally unsuitable *ch* symbol, as in *chutzpa* and *Chanuka*, which many non-Jews thus pronounce erroneously with the initial sound of *chin*. The digraph *ch* is especially unsuitable for words such as the aforegoing, which derive ultimately from ancient Hebrew rather than German. Even the awkward-looking and hypercorrect *ḥ* used by Hebrew scholars to transliterate the letter *khet* (as distinguished from the letter *khaf*, which they render *kh*) is linguistically more acceptable than the use of *ch*. I am of course aware that *ch* is commonly used in Israel (where German-speaking Jews have long been influential) as a suitable symbol for [x] in romanizing Hebrew words. I would still recommend that this confusing and unnecessary symbol be eradicated from the transcription of Jewish-origin terms. See also my objection to the spelling *sch* on similar grounds (Chapter 5, note 16).

The remaining few distinctive consonants, vowels, and diphthongs in the transcription key pose no difficulty. The system follows the pronunciation of Standard Yiddish and requires no special knowledge of the Yiddish spelling. The novice in Yiddish may wish to note only that Yiddish, like Hebrew, does not contain capital letters, so that an exact transcription from Yiddish should be without capitals. Nevertheless, certain conventions have developed in this respect: the beginning of a romanized sentence is usually capitalized, and so are proper names; in titles, sometimes only the first word is capitalized, thus: *Geshikhte fun der yidisher shprakh* (History of the Yiddish Language).

Transcription Key for Yiddish into Roman Letters

אַ	a	—	אַנדערש	andersh
אָ	o	—	גאָט	got
ב	b	—	פּראָבלעם	problem
בֿ	v	—	מקרבֿ	mekarev
ג	g	—	גאָר	gor
ד	d	—	דאָס	dos
ה	h	—	האָבן	hobn
ו	u	—	קומען	kumen
וו	v	—	ווען	ven
וי	oy	—	קוימען	koymen
ז	z	—	אַזוי	azoy
זש	zh	—	זשאַבע	zhabe
ח	kh	—	חוץ	khuts
ט	t	—	טאַנץ	tants
טש	tsh	—	מוטשען	mutshen
יִ,י	i	—	טיש,רויִק	tish, ruik
	y	—	יאָר,ייד	yor, yid
			ייִדיש	yidish
			יעדער	yeder
יי	ey	—	גיין	geyn

יַי	ay —	גלייַך	glaykh
כ,ך	kh —	כאַפּן,סך	khapn, sakh
כּ	k —	כּלה	kale
ל	l —	ליבע	libe
מ,ם	m —	מענטש	mentsh
		קום	kum
נ,ן	n —	נעכטן	nekhtn
ס	s —	סמך	smakh
ע	e —	עסן	esn
פּ	p —	פּוילן	poyln
פֿ,ף	f —	פֿאַקט, לויף	fakt, loyf
צ,ץ	ts —	צוריק	tsurik
		זאַץ	zats
ק	k —	קולטור	kultur
ר	r —	רעוואָלוציע	revolutsye
שׁ	sh —	שיין	sheyn
שׂ	s —	שׂרה	sore
תּ	t —	תּוך	tokh
ת	s —	טעות	toes

Consonants

The consonants are the same as in English except for the following (corresponding IPA symbols are given in brackets):

kh	as in Scottish loch	[x]
sh	as in shy	[ʃ]
tsh	as in chair, watch	[tʃ]

ts	as in hats, Ritz	[ts]
zh	as in azure, treasure	[ʒ]

There are five vowels and three diphthongs, as follows:

Vowels

a	as in ah, car, calm	[ɑ]
e	as in red, ten, set	[ɛ]

(pronounced even as the last letter of a word)

i	as in hit, fit, tin	[ɪ]

(except at the end of a word where it is
pronounced as in English *see, even,* etc. [i])

o	as in lord, tall	[ɔ]
u	as in put, foot	[ʊ]

(rarely, also as in English rule, tool [u])

Diphthongs

ay	as in lie, guy	[ɑɪ]
ey	as in day, ape	[e]
oy	as in oil, boy	[ɔɪ]

Appendix II:
A Glossary of Jewish English

This glossary is a selection of some twelve hundred words, phrases, and idioms of mostly Eastern Yiddish and Modern Hebrew origin which appear frequently in the English writings and speech of American Ashkenazic Jews of East European origin or descent. A certain number of these usages occur with special frequency among the Modern Orthodox Ashkenazic Jews whose form of Jewish English is discussed in Chapter 6, but it can be assumed that most of the entries in the glossary are known in varying degrees to the larger grouping of Ashkenazic Jews of this country. The selection is based on several thousand citations which I have extracted over a period of about ten years from English-language periodicals and books of the American Jewish community, as well as on usages recorded from the talk of Jewish-English speakers.

The purpose of this glossary is to list those usages of Yiddish and Hebrew origin that usually go unlisted in glossaries of "Jewish" terms, which include as a rule only the well-known religious and traditional vocabulary of Judaism (see, for example, the glossary at the beginning of each volume of the *Encyclopaedia Judaica*). But while a certain number of the entries in this glossary can also be found in various "Yinglish" types of humorous dictionaries designed for popular entertainment, they are usually so badly mangled in spelling and definition that this glossary, though far from being perfect or complete and hardly a dictionary, can serve as a useful corrective to the shortcomings and excesses of those "dictionaries."

In general, this glossary includes chiefly "common vocabulary" items, omitting such categories as the names of foods and dishes (of which there are hundreds), and the names of ceremonial objects, rituals, holidays, months of the year, prayers and blessings, communal functions and functionaries, political and social organizations, historical events, and the like. When it does include a specifically religious or ritualistic term, it is usually for comparative or contrastive purposes; thus *aliye* is entered because its doublet *aliya* is. But even for the "common vocabulary" this selection is limited to a sampling of the actual common stock of lexemes available to many Jewish-English users; for example, the glossary includes *yid, pintele yid, yidene*, and *yidishkayt*, but omits *yidish, yidele* 'Jew' (endearing), *sheyner yid* 'fine Jew,' and other familiar expressions built around the word *yid*. No doubt a larger book could include twice as many Yiddishisms and Hebraisms as are contained here.

As explained in Appendix I, the Yiddish-origin entries are transcribed according to the (morphophonemic) YIVO transcription system, formerly also known as the American National Standard Romanization of Yiddish. The entries derived from Modern Hebrew are transcribed according to the system of the American National Standard Romanization of Hebrew, with one exception: the spirant [x] is transcribed with the digraph *kh* rather than *ch*, as in *khag sameakh* (not *chag sameach*). I have done this partly on the grounds that I consider the German orthographic symbol *ch* unsuitable where the more scholarly symbol *kh* is available, and partly to bring the romanization of Yiddish and Hebrew closer to each other. This seems to me a desirable goal, if for no other reason than that the two languages have many words which are spelled exactly alike, and it would seem logical that their romanized forms should retain the similarity (e.g., Hebrew *takhlit*, Yiddish *takhles*, Hebrew *bakhur*, Yiddish *bokher*) wherever possible.

The transcriptions of Yiddish-origin words in the Glossary generally represent the pronunciation of Standard Yiddish, which resembles most closely the Northeastern Yiddish pronunciation. However, in a few cases, a frequently encountered dialectal variant is also listed (e.g., *hunt/hint, mume/mime*). In order to avoid the complication of intrusive markings, no stress marks are given to the forms. Normally in Yiddish-origin words of more than one syllable, the stress falls on the penultimate or next-to-the-last syllable: *balego'le, blo'te, aley'khem sho'lem.* But in many instances the stress is on the last syllable, as it is usually in Hebrew: *ahin', haklal', halevay',* etc. A characteristic difference between the Yiddish and Hebrew stress systems is illustrated by the doublets *aliye/aliya,* the former being pronounced *ali'ye,* the latter *aliya'* (as in *to get an ali'ye* and *to make aliya'*).

The bulk of the entries are from Eastern Yiddish (one form, *nebish,* is from Western Yiddish). Words taken from American Yiddish are so indicated in parenthesis at the end of the entry, thus: *boytshik . . .* (Am. Yid.). Words borrowed from Modern Hebrew are similarly indicated: *dati . . .* (Mod. Heb.).

abba, *n.* father; daddy. (Mod. Heb.)
abi, *adv.* provided (that); at least.
abi gezunt, the most important thing is health.
aderabe, *adv.* on the contrary; not at all.
afile, *adv.* even.
agmes nefesh, anxiety; vexation; grief.
agune, *n.* deserted wife.
ahave, *n.* love.
aher, *adv.* here; to here.
ahin, *adv.* there; to there.
akhdes, *n.* unity.
akhrayes, *n.* responsibility.
akhren akhren khoviv, (saving) the best for last.
aklal, *adv.* = haklal.
akshn, *n.* stubborn person.
akshones, *n.* stubbornness.
alef-beys, *n.* the Jewish alphabet.
alevay, *interj.* = halevay.
aleykhem sholem, unto you peace (greeting said in response to *sholem aleykhem*).
aliya, *n.* immigration to Israel. Cf. **ole.** (Mod. Heb.)
aliye, *n.* honor of being called up to the Torah-reading desk.
almen, *n.* widower.
almone, *n.* widow.
al regel akhas, briefly; in a nutshell; *lit.,* on one foot.

alte moyd, spinster; *lit.,* old maid.

alter bokher, bachelor; *lit.,* old lad.

alter terakh, old fool; *lit.,* old Terakh (father of the patriarch Abraham).

ameratses, *n.* ignorance, esp. of Judaism.

amorets, *n., pl.* **ameratsim.** ignoramus; boor.

anives, *n.* humility. Cf. **onev.**

antisemit, *n., fem.* **antisemitke.** anti-Semite. Cf. **roshe.**

apikoyres, *n., pl.* **apikorsim.** unbeliever; heretic; freethinker.

arayngefaln, *adj.* deceived; *lit.,* fallen in.

arayngezogt, *adj.* told off; rebuked.

arbes, *n.* chickpeas.

arop, *adv.* off; down.

aroys, *adj., interj.* out.

aroysgevorfn, *adj.* wasted; vain; useless; *lit.,* thrown out.

aroysgevorfene gelt, wasted or squandered money.

aruf, *adv.* up.

arum, *adv.* around.

ashires, *n.* wealth.

make ash un blote from, make mincemeat of; *lit.,* make ashes and mud from.

avade, *adv.* certainly; surely.

avek, *adv.* away; off.

aveyre, *n.* sin. Also, **neveyre.**

avle, *n.* injustice; grievance.

ay-ay-ay, *interj., adj.* wonderful; terrific.

aynfal, *n.* idea; notion.

ayn hore, evil eye. See **kanehore.**

aynredenish, *n.* self-delusion; fantasy.

a yor mit a mitvokh, a long time; *lit.,* a year and a Wednesday.

aza yor af mir, it should happen to me; *lit.,* such a year upon me.

azes, *n.* insolence; impudence.

azes ponim, brazen, impudent person.

azeskayt, *n.* − azes.

azoy, *adv.* so; thus.

azoyns un azelekhes, something very special; exquisite; *lit.,* such and such.

bagrobn, *adj.* buried (*lit.* and *fig.*).

bakante(r), *n.* acquaintance.
bakoshe, *n.* favor.
bakvem, *adj.* comfortable; cozy.
balebatim, *n.* plural of **balebos.**
balebatish, *adj.* respectable; proper; genteel.
balebos, *n.* **1.** head of a household. **2.** owner; proprietor; landlord. **3.** member of a congregation. **4.** layman.
baleboste, *n.* feminine of **balebos. 1.** mistress of a household. **2.** hostess; housekeeper; housewife. **3.** landlady.
balegole, *n.* common, coarse person; *lit.*, wagon driver; coachman.
baleydikt, *adj.* insulted.
bal gayve, conceited person.
balmelokhe, *n.* worker; craftsman.
bal pe, by heart; orally.
bal simkhe, celebrant; sponsor of a celebration.
bal tshuve, penitent Jew; Jew who has turned religious.
bal tsdoke, charitable person.
bashefer, *n.* Creator.
bashert, *adj.* predestined.
basherte(r), *n.* predestined mate. Cf. **zivig.**
bashtimt, *adj.* definite; set; certain.
bas yekhide, only daughter. Cf. **ben yokhid.**
batamt, *adj.* **1.** tasty; delicious. **2.** cute. Cf. ¹**tam.**
batlen, *n., pl.* **batlonim. 1.** idle person; loafer. **2.** naive, impractical person. Cf. **bitl.**
bavust, *adj.* well-known; eminent.
bay laytn(s), among fine, respectable people.
bays, *n., v.* bite.
bayshn, *n., pl.* **bayshonim.** bashful person.
beheyme, *n.* **1.** cow; animal. **2.** fool; idiot.
beheymish, *adj.* foolish; idiotic.
bekhine, *n.* **1.** category; level. **2.** examination (in Jewish subject).
bekhire, *n.* freedom of choice; free will.
bekitser, *adv.* in short; briefly.
bekies, *n.* proficiency; adeptness. Cf. **boki.**
bekovedik, *adj.* dignified; respectable.
belaaz, *adv.* **1.** in the vernacular or foreign language (i.e., not Hebrew or Yiddish). **2.** also known as; alias.

beli guzme, without exaggeration; really.

beli neyder, no vow intended (said of a future action, promise, etc.).

benemones, *adv.* honestly.

ben yokhid, only son. Cf. **bas yekhide.**

beerekh, *adv.* approximately; roughly.

berye, *n.* a very competent woman.

beshas mayse, at the time.

besod soydes, very secretly.

besoylem, *n.* Jewish cemetery.

bevakasha, *adv.* please. (Mod. Heb.)

beynashmoshes, *n.* twilight.

beys mayse, at the (same) time.

beyz, *adj.* angry.

beze haloshn, as follows.

bifrat, *adv.* particularly; in particular.

biker khoylim, visiting the sick.

bilbl, *n.* calumny; libel.

bilik, *adj.* cheap; *fig.* **bilik vi borsht,** dirt cheap.

bishtike, *adv.* quietly; silently; stealthily.

bisl, *n.* bit; little.

bislekhvays, *adv.* gradually; bit by bit.

bitl, *n.* **1.** contempt; disparagement. Cf. **mevatl. 2.** also **bitl zman.** waste of time; idleness. Cf. **batlen.**

bitokhn, *n.* trust; faith.

biz hundert un tsvantsik, till 120 years (a birthday greeting).

bizoyen, *n.* shame; disgrace.

blondzhe, *v.* stray; ramble. Cf. **farblondzhet.**

blote, *n.* mud; filth (*lit.* and *fig.*).

bobe, *n.* grandmother.

bobe mayse, old wives' tale; tall tale.

bobes tam, bad taste; tasteless; inferior; *lit.*, grandmother's taste.

bobkes, *n.* beans; chicken feed; *lit.*, sheep or goat dung.

boki, *adj.* proficient; adept.—*n., pl.* **bekiim.** person who is proficient.

bokher, *n.* lad; youth; young man.

borkhabe, borukh habo, welcome.

borves, *adj.* barefoot.

botl, *adj.* null; void. Cf. **oyverbotl.**

118   APPENDIX II

boydem, *n.* attic.
boykh, *n.* stomach.
boykhveytik, *n.* stomachache (*lit.* and *fig.*).
boytshik, *n.* young boy; young fellow. (Am. Yid.)
boytshikl, *n.* diminutive of **boytshik.**
brekl, *n., pl.* **breklekh.** scrap; crumb; bit.
bren, *n.* spirited person; livewire; *lit.,* a burn.
breyre, *n.* choice; alternative.
brider, *n.* = bruder.
brokh, *n.* misfortune; *lit.,* break; crack.
a brokh is mir, woe is me.
brokhe, *n.* blessing; boon.
brokhe levatole, a waste; *lit.,* wasted blessing.
bronfn, *n.* whiskey.
broygez, *adj.* sore; angry.
bruder, *n.* brother.
bsure, *n.* announcement; news.
bube, *n.* = bobe.
bubele, *n.* darling; sweetheart; *lit.,* little grandmother.
bulvan, *n.* goon; oaf.
burtshe, *v.* grumble.
dafke, *adv.* precisely; necessarily; purposely.
dales, *n.* poverty; squalor.
dalfn, *n.* pauper. (from the name of *Dalfon,* one of the sons of
    Haman who was hanged, by influence of Hebrew *dal* 'poor.')
darshn, *n.* preacher; orator. Cf. **droshe.**
dati, *adj.* religious; Orthodox.—*n., pl.* **datiyim.** religious Jew.
    (Mod. Heb.)
dayge, *n.* worry; problem.
derekh erets, manners; courtesy; respect.
dergey di yorn, pester; annoy; *lit.,* trample the years.
dervayle, *adv.* meanwhile.
deyfek, *n.* pulse.
dibuk, *n.* demon; evil spirit or soul that enters a living person.
din vekhezhbn, accounting; reckoning.
dinst, *n.* maidservant.
dire, *n.* apartment; dwelling.
dirigir, *v.* control; direct.

dor, *n.* generation.

dover akher, 1. abomination. **2.** scoundrel. **3.** swine. **4.** (*lit.*) other thing.

drey arum, run around.

drey a kop, muddle (one) up; pester; *lit.*, twist a head.

drey a spodik, pester; annoy; *lit.*, twirl a high fur hat.

dreykop, *n.* **1.** flighty person. **2.** nuisance; pest. **3.** schemer.

driml, *v., n.* doze; nap.

droshe, *n.* sermon; speech.

droshe geshank, wedding present.

durkhgetribn, *adj.* shrewd; crafty.

dveykes, *n.* religious ecstasy.

efsher, *adv.* maybe.

ek, *n.* end; extremity.

ekl, *v.* disgust.

ekldik, *adj.* disgusting.

ek velt, end of the world.

-ele, diminutive suffix added to nouns, as in *bubele.* (second-degree variant of **-l**).

emes, *n.* truth.—*adj.* true.

emes velt, the next world; the hereafter; *lit.*, true world.

emesdik, *adj.* truthful; genuine.

emetser, *pron.* somebody.

emune, *n.* (Jewish) faith or creed.

epes, *adv.* somewhat.—*pron.* something; anything.

erd, *n.* earth; ground.

erev, *prep.* before; on the eve of.

erlekh, *adj.* honest; sincere.

es, *v., interj.* eat.

eydem, *n.* son-in-law.

eydl, *adj.* delicate; refined.

eyn hokhi nami, granted; to be sure. (Yid. < Aram.)

eynikl, *n., pl.* **eyniklekh.** grandchild.

eyshes khayil, woman of valor; good wife.

eytse, *n.* advice.

fang shoyn on, begin already; start up.

farbayt di yoytsres, confuse things.

farbisn, *adj.* mean; dour; truculent.

farbisene(r), *n.* mean, truculent person.
farbitert, *adj.* embittered.
farblondzhet, *adj.* lost; gone astray.
farbreng, *v.* 1. spend or pass time. 2. take part in a Hasidic get-together.
farbrente(r), *adj.* ardent; zealous.
fardorbn, *adj.* spoiled; depraved; corrupt.
farfaln, *adj.* lost; hopeless.—*interj.* no use; it's a lost cause.
farfl, *n.* noodle pellets.
farfoylt, *adj.* rotten.
fargenign, *n.* pleasure; delight.
fargesn, *adj.* forgotten.
fargin, *v.* not begrudge.
farher, *n.* interrogation; examination.
farkert, *adj.* opposite; reverse.
farkrimt, *adj.* distorted; twisted.
farmatert, *adj.* tired; weary.
farmeygn, *n.* large fortune.
farmisht, *adj.* mixed up; confused.
farpatshket, *adj.* messed up. Cf. **patshke.**
farplonter, *v.* entangle; muddle.
farputst, *adj.* = oysgeputst.
farshlept, *adj.* drawn or dragged out. Cf. **shlep.**
farshlepte krenk, 1. long, drawn-out story, etc. 2. obnoxious person. 3. (*lit.*) drawn-out illness.
farshlofener, *n.* dull-witted person; sleepyhead.
farshter, *v.* spoil; mar; frustrate.
farshtey, *v.* understand.
farshtey a krenk, understand nothing; *lit.*, understand a sickness.
farshtunken, *adj.* stinking.
farshvitst, *adj.* sweated up.
fartshadet, *adj.* confused; dazed; stunned.
fartumlt, *adj.* = tsutumlt.
fayf, *v.* whistle; boo.
fayfer, *n.* uncouth, conceited person; *lit.*, whistler.
fe, *interj.* expression of disgust; ugh.
ferd, *n.* fool; dumbbell; *lit.*, horse. Cf. **beheyme, hunt.**
feter, *n.* uncle.

finster, *adj.* dark.

finsterer sof, disaster; ruin; *lit.*, dark ending.

fleysh, *n.* meat; flesh.

fleyshik, *adj.* made of meat.

folg mir a gang, it's a long distance; *fig.*, far be it from me; not a chance.

fonfe, *v.* talk with a nasal twang; hem and haw; bluff.

fonfer, *n.* double-talker; bluffer; phoney.

foyl, *adj.* **1.** lazy; sluggish. **2.** rotten; putrid.

foyler, *n.* lazy person; sluggard.

frask, *n.* slap; smack.

freg mikh bekheyrem, I don't have the slightest idea; *lit.*, (it's as if you) ask me (while) under a ban. Cf. **kheyrem.**

freg nisht, don't ask.

fres, *v.* gorge oneself on food; devour.

freser, *n.* glutton.

freylekh, *adj.* merry; cheerful.

freylekhs, *n.* **1.** cheerful tune. **2.** Jewish folk dance.

frum, *adj.* religious.

gadles, *n.* greatness; *also,* conceit.

galekh, *n.* priest or minister; non-Jewish clergyman.

galut, *n.* = goles. (Mod. Heb.)

gam atem, same to you (response to good wishes).

gam zu letoyve, it's all for the best; *lit.*, this, too, is for the best.

ganef, *n.* **1.** thief. **2.** rascal.

gan eydn, paradise; heaven; *lit.*, garden of Eden.

ganeyve, *n.* theft; robbery.

ganeyvish, *adj.* thievish; sneaky.

gantse(r), *adj.* complete; thorough.

garin, *n.* group or unit; *lit.*, kernel, nucleus. (Mod. Heb.)

gartl, *n.* sash or belt, esp. of a Hasidic Jew.

gatkes, *n.* underpants.

gashmies, *n.* materiality; worldliness. Cf. **rukhnies.**

gayve, *n.* conceit; arrogance.

gazlen, *n., pl.* **gazlonim.** robber; bandit; swindler.

gdule, *n.* big celebration; big deal (ironic).

gebentsht, *adj.* blessed.

gedeyrem, *n. pl.* bowels; intestines.

geduld, *n.* patience.
geferlekh, *adj.* dangerous; terrible.
gefil, *n.* feeling.
gehakte tsores, great troubles; miserable state; *lit.*, chopped troubles.
gehenem, *n.* hell.
gelekhter, *n.* laugh; laughter; laughing.
gelt, *n.* money.
gelungen, *adj.* successful.
gemeyn, *adj.* common; coarse; vile.
gemeyner yung, coarse fellow.
genung, *adj.* enough.
gepokt un gemozlt, experienced; wordly-wise; *lit.*, poxed and measled (gone through childhood diseases).
ger, *n.* convert to Judaism.
gerotn, *adj.* good-looking; fair.
gesheft, *n.* business.
geshikhte, *n.* history; story.
geshmak, *adj.* tasty; delicious.—*n.* taste; gusto.
geshmadt, *adj.* converted from Judaism. Cf. **shmad, meshumed.**
geshrey, *n.* shout; yell.
get, *n.* divorce.
geule, *n.* redemption; salvation.
gevald, *n., interj.* **1.** hue and cry; alarm. **2.** violence; force.
gevaldeve, *v.* scream; rant; rave.
gevaldik, *adj.* extraordinary; terrific.
geveyn, *n.* weeping; lament.
gey, *v.* go.
gey avek, go away.
gey in drerd, go to the devil; *lit.*, go into the ground (drerd = der erd).
gezunt, *n.* health.
gezunterheyt, *adv.* in good health.
gilgl, *n.* reincarnation; transformation (also *fig.*).
glat, *adj.* **1.** smooth; slick. **2.** flawless; strictly kosher.
glat azoy, just like that; for no good reason.
glet, *v.* caress; stroke.
glik, *n.* good luck; great fortune (often ironic).

gliklekh, *adj.* happy.
glitsh, *v., n.* slip; skid; skate.
gmiles khesed, interest-free loan.
godl, *n., pl.* **gdoylim.** prominent man, esp. a great scholar.
goen, *n., pl.* **geoynim.** great scholar; genius.
gola, *n.* = goles. (Mod. Heb.)
goldene medine, America; *lit.*, golden country.
goles, *n.* exile; diaspora.
gorgl, *n.* throat; gullet.
gornisht, *adj.* nothing.
gornisht mit gornisht, (worth) absolutely nothing.
got, *n.* God.
got di neshome shuldik, appearing completely innocent; *lit.*, (acting as though he) owes his soul to God.
gotenyu, *interj.* dear God.
gots politsey, social censor; self-appointed moral arbiter; *lit.*, God's police.
got tsu danken, thank God.
got zol ophitn, God forbid.
goy, *n.* non-Jewish male.
goyder, *n.* double chin.
goye, *n.* non-Jewish female.
goyish, *adj.* non-Jewish.
goylem, *n.* **1.** clumsy person; dummy. Cf. **leymener goylem. 2.** a golem (artificial creature formed from clay by kabbalistic means).
goyrl, *n.* fate; lot; destiny.
goyses, *n.* dying person.
gramen, *n. pl.* improvised rhyming verses, as at a wedding; *lit.*, rhyming.
grepts, *n., v.* belch.
grine(r), *n.* greenhorn.
gring, *adj.* easy.
grizhe, *v.* gnaw; nag.
grob, *adj.* thick; fat; (fig.) boorish; coarse.
grober yung, coarse, ignorant fellow; ignoramus; boor.
grobyan, *n.* coarse, vulgar person.
grushe, *n.* divorcée.

gufe, *adv.* in person.

gut, *adj.* good.

guter bruder, buddy; comrade; *lit.*, good brother.

gut gezogt, well said.

gut vokh, good week (greeting at conclusion of Sabbath).

gut yontev, happy holiday.

gut yor, good year; happy new year.

guzme, *n.* exaggeration.

gvir, *n.* rich man.

gzeyle, *n.* robbery.

gzeyre, *n.* **1.** evil decree. **2.** (in Jewish law) rabbinical prohibition.

hafsoke, *n.* interruption; break.

hak, *n.* violent blow; stroke.—*v.* strike; beat; hit.

hak a tshaynik, babble nonsense; *lit.*, beat a teakettle.

hakhnose, *n.* income.

hakhnoses orkhim, hospitality.

hakhshara, *n.* training camp (or period) for Zionist youth. (Mod. Heb.)

hakitser, *adv.* in short; in a word.

haklal, *adv.* in short. Also, **aklal.**

hakol beseder, all is well; *lit.*, everything is in order. (Mod. Heb.)

halevay, *interj.* would that it be so. Also, **alevay.**

halt zikh ba di zaytn, split one's sides (laughing); be in stitches.

hamoyn am, populace; the masses.

handl, *n.* business; trade.

hashgokhe, *n.* **1.** Providence. **2.** rabbinic supervision.

hashkofe, *n.* view; outlook; attitude.

hashpoe, *n.* influence. Cf. **mashpie.**

haskome, *n.* consent; approval. Cf. **maskim.**

hasmode, *n.* diligence or industry, esp. in study.

hatslokhe, *n.* good fortune; success.

have in the linke(r) pyate, not give a hoot; *lit.*, have in the left heel.

hayitokhn, *interj.* how come.

hefker, *adj.* **1.** ownerless. **2.** lawless; unruly.

hefker petrishke, anything goes; *lit.*, ownerless parsley.

hefkeyres, *n.* abandonment; lawlessness.

hekhsher, *n.* permission; approval (especially rabbinic).

helf (or **help**) **vi a toytn bankes,** be totally useless or ineffective; *lit.*, help as cupping (helps) a corpse.

hesder, *n.* program in Israel combining yeshiva study and military service. (Mod. Heb.)

hesped, *n.* funeral oration or eulogy.

heter, *n.* legal permission; lenient ruling.

heymish, *adj.* homelike; cozy; familiar.

heypekh, *n.* opposite; contrary.

hezek, *n.* damage; loss.

hinkedik, *adj.* lame; limping.

hint, *n.* = hunt.

hislayves, *n.* fervor; ecstasy.

hits, *n.* heat; hot spell.

hitsik, *adj.* hot-headed; impetuous.

hitsiker, *n.* impetuous person.

hob in drerd, not give a hoot for; *lit.*, have in the ground (drerd = der erd).

hob (or **have**) **tsu zingen un tsu zogn,** have no end of trouble; *lit.*, have to sing and to say.

hodeve, *v.* bring up; raise.

holdopnik, *n.* bandit; thief. (Am. Yid. < Eng. *hold up*)

horeve, *v.* toil; drudge.

hoyker, *n.* hunchback; hump.

hoytsoes, *n. pl.* expenses.

hu-ha, *n.* hullaballoo; fuss; bustle.

hulyanke, *n.* revel; spree.

hunt, *n.* dog (*lit.* and *fig.*) Cf. **kelev.**

iberkerenish, *n.* upheaval; upset.

iberkhazer, *v.* repeat; review.

iberyor, *n.* leap year.

ikh veys, do I know; how should I know.

iker, *n.* essence; basic principle.

ile, *n.* young genius; prodigy.

imma, *n.* mother; mommy. (Mod. Heb.)

in drerd, finished; done for; *lit.*, in the ground (drerd = der erd).

in mitn drinen, in the middle of everything; suddenly.

inyen, *n., pl.* **inyonim.** matter; affair.

iser, *n.* legal prohibition; strict ruling.

Ivrit, *n.* Modern Hebrew. (Mod. Heb.)

kaas, *n.* anger.

kaboles ponim, reception; welcome.

kabtsn, *n.* poor man; pauper.

kadokhes, *n.* fever (used as a curse); *also,* a jeer, = less than nothing.

kale, *n.* bride.

kalike, *n.* cripple (*lit.* and *fig.*).

kalye, *adj.* spoiled; out of order.

kameye, *n.* amulet.

kamtsn, *n.* stingy person; miser.

kanehore, *adv.* may no evil eye befall; knock on wood. Cf. **ayn hore.**

kanoy, *n.* zealot; fanatic.

kantshik, *n.* whip.

kapelye, *n.* musical band.

kapitl, *n.* chapter.

kapore, *n.* scapegoat; *fig.*, punishment; atonement.

kapoyer, *adj.* topsy-turvy. Cf. **moyshe kapoyer.**

karg, *adj.* stingy.

karger, *n.* stingy person.

karke, *n.* cemetery plot.

kas, *n.* = kaas.

¹kashe, *n.* question; difficulty. (Yid. < Heb.)

²kashe, *n.* groats; porridge. (Yid. < Slav.)

kavone, *n.* **1.** devotion; fervor. **2.** intent.

kavyokhl, *adv.* as if; as though possible (when used in reference to God, a euphemism for the Divine Name).

kayn ayn hore = kanehore.

keday, *adv.* worthwhile; advisable.

kehile, *n.* Jewish community or congregation.

kelev, *n.* vicious dog; cur (*lit.* and *fig.*).

keshene, *n.* pocket; *fig.*, pocketbook.

keshene gelt, pocket money.

kest, *n.* room and board; keep (esp. of a son-in-law).

keyle, *n., pl.* **keylim.** vessel; dish; instrument.

keyn yirbu, may they increase in numbers.

keyver, *n.* grave; tomb.

kfar, *n.* Israeli village. (Mod. Heb.)
khabar, *n.* bribe; graft.
khagige, *n.* festival; celebration.
khag sameakh, happy holiday (Mod. Heb.)
khalesh, *v.* faint.
khaloshes, *n.* nausea; repugnant thing.
khaloshesdik, *adj.* disgusting; nauseating.
khanfe, *v.* flatter.
khanife, *n.* flattery.
khanukas habayis, dedication of a house or building;
  housewarming.
khap, *v.* catch.
khapenish, *n.* rush; haste.
khaplap, *adv.* haphazardly; helter-skelter.
khared, *n., pl.* **kharedim.** ultra-Orthodox Jew. (Mod. Heb.)
kharote, *n.* regret; repentance.
kharpe, *n.* shame; disgrace.
khasene, *n.* wedding.
khas vekholile, heaven forbid.
khas vesholem, heaven forbid.
khaver, *n., fem.* **khaverte.** friend; companion; comrade.
khavura, *n.* society; fellowship. (Mod. Heb.)
khaye, *n.* beast (*lit.* and *fig.*).
khayev, *adj.* guilty; responsible.
khazer, *n.* pig; *fig.*, glutton.
khazeray, *n.* filth; mess; trashy food.
khazerish, *adj.* swinish; filthy.
khesed, *n.* mercy; grace; favor.
kheshbn, *n.* reckoning; calculation.
khevre, *n.* society; close-knit group (of friends).
khevreman, *n., pl.* **khevrelayt.** fellow; guy, esp. a tough guy;
  person hard to get along with.
kheylek, *n.* part; share.
kheyn, *n.* grace; charm.
kheynevdik, *adj.* charming.
kheyrem, *n.* ban; excommunication; ostracism.
kheyshek, *n.* desire; eagerness.
khidesh, *n.* **1.** novelty. **2.** novella. **3.** surprise.

khilek, *n.* difference.

khisorn, *n.* fault; defect; flaw.

khiyev, *n.* responsibility; obligation.

khnyok, *n.* **1.** narrow-minded person; bigot. **2.** slob; uncouth fellow.

khnyokish, *adj.* bigoted.

khoge, *n.* non-Jewish holiday.

khokhem, *n.* smart person; wise man (often ironic, esp. in **khokhem eyner,** smart one, fool).

khokhme, *n.* clever act or saying; witticism; *also,* wisdom.

kholem, *n., pl.* **khaloymes.** dream.

kholerye, *n.* cholera; plague (used as a curse).

kholile, *adv.* heaven forbid.

khorev, *adj.* destroyed; ruined.

khoshev, *adj.* prominent; respected; important.

khosn, *n.* bridegroom.

khotsh, khotshe, *adv.* at least; although.

khoyle, *n.* sick person; patient.

be khoyshed, *v.* suspect.

khoyshekh, *n.* darkness (*lit.* and *fig.*).

khoyv, *n.* debt; duty.

khoyzek, *n.* ridicule.

khozrim, *n. pl.* returnees to Israel from abroad. Cf. **olim, noshrim, yordim.** (Mod. Heb.)

khreyn, *n.* horseradish.

khrop, *v.* snore.

khshad, *n.* suspicion.

khug, *n.* circle; club. (Mod. Heb.)

khupe, *n.* wedding ceremony or canopy.

khurbn, *n.* ruin; destruction; *also,* the Holocaust. Cf. **shoa.**

khush, *n.* sense; feeling; flair.

khutspe, *n.* **1.** impertinence; impudence; nerve. **2.** outrageous impudence; brazen gall.

khutspedik, *adj.* having khutspe; impertinent; brazen; cocky.

kibud, *n.* **1.** *pl.* **kibudim.** honor. **2.** reverence. **3.** refreshments.

kikhl, *n., pl.* **kikhlekh.** cookie.

kile, *n.* hernia.

kimat, *adv.* almost; nearly; virtually.

kind, *n.* child.

kinder, *n. pl.* (diminutive **kinderlekh**) children.
kine, *n.* envy; jealousy.
kine-sine, *n.* rivalry.
kishef, *n.* magic; witchcraft.
kishke, *n.* **1.** gut; intestine (*lit.* and *fig.*). **2.** stuffed derma.
kishn, *n.* pillow.
kita, *n.* section; class (in school). (Mod. Heb.)
kite, *n.* faction; party.
kitsl, *v., n.* tickle.
kiyem, *n.* continued existence; survival.
klal, *n.* community.
klal tuer, community leader.
klap, *n., pl.* **klep.** stroke; hit; blow.
kleynikayt, *n.* trifle.
klezmer, *n.* **1.** traditional Ashkenazic musician or band. **2.** music
    played by a klezmer. (Yid. < Heb., musical instruments)
klipe, *n.* **1.** nag; shrew. **2.** evil spirit.
klita, *n.* absorption of immigrants in Israel. (Mod. Heb.)
a klog (tsu), *n.* **1.** woe (to); damn. **2.** lament.
klole, *n.* curse.
klop, *n.* = klap.
klor, *adj.* clear.
klots, *n.* clumsy person.
klots kashe, naive or unintelligent question.
kloymersht, *adv.* as it were; ostensibly.
kloyster, *n.* church.
klug, *adj.* smart; wise.
knaker, *n.* **1.** big wheel; big shot. **2.** wise guy; know-it-all.
knaper, *adj.* slight; not much of.
kneytsh, *n.* crease.
knip, *n.* pinch; nip.
kokhlefl, *n.* busybody; meddler; *lit.*, cooking spoon.
knipl, *n.* savings; nest egg.
kolboynik, *n.* **1.** jack of all trades. **2.** rascal.
kol, *n.* voice.
kol hakavod, all honor (to a person); well done. (Mod. Heb.)
kol tuv, all the best (greeting).
konkurent, *n.* competitor; rival.

kop, *n., pl.* **kep.** head.
kopdreyenish, *n.* nuisance; headache; *lit.*, head spinning. Cf.
    dreykop.
korbn, *n.* sacrifice.
korev, *n., pl.* **kroyvim.** relative; kin.
koved, *n.* honor; glory; testimonial.
koydem, *adv.* first.
koydem kol, first of all.
koyekh, *n.* strength.
koym, *adv.* barely; scarcely.
koyne, *n.* customer.
krank, *adj.* sick.
krats, *v.* scratch.
krekhts, *v., n.* groan; complain(t).
krenk, *n.* sickness (often *fig.*).
kreplekh, *n. pl.* boiled stuffed dumplings.
krikh, *v.* crawl.
ksav yad, manuscript.
kumzits, *n.* campfire gathering; *lit.*, come-sit.
kunts, *n., pl.* **kuntsn.** Stunt; feat; trick.
kvater, *n.* godfather.
kvel, *v.* be delighted (with); revel in.
kvetsh, *v.* complain; find fault; *lit.*, squeeze; pinch.—*n.* habitual
    complainer or faultfinder.
kvitsh, *n., v.* scream.
kvutsa, *n.* agricultural collective in Israel. (Mod. Heb.)
-l, diminutive suffix added to nouns, as in *tsigaretl* 'little cigarette,'
    boytshikl 'little boytshik.'
labriut, *interj.* = tsu gezunt. (Mod. Heb.)
lager, *n.* concentration camp.
lamdn, *n.* Talmudic scholar.
lamed-vovnik, *n.* hidden saint; *lit.*, one of thirty-six righteous men
    of Jewish tradition (*lamed* '30' + *vov* '6').
landslayt, *n. pl.* landsmen; fellow townsmen or countrymen.
landsmanshaft, *n.* association of landslayt.
late, *n.* patch.
laykhter, *n.* candlestick.
laytish, *adj.* proper; respectable.

lebedik, *adj.* lively.

lebediker, *n.* lively person.

a lebn af dir, bless you! (after a sneeze, etc.); *lit.*, life upon you.

lehakhes, *n.* spite. Cf. **tsulokhes, oyf tsulokhes.**

lehakhesdik, *adj.* spiteful.

lehakhesnik, *n.* spiteful person.

lehavdl, *adv.* no comparison intended; *lit.*, to divide, separate (esp. between sacred and profane).

lehitraot, *interj.* till we meet again; au revoir. (Mod. Heb.)

lekekh, *n.* cake, esp. honey or sponge cake.

lekhayim, *interj.* to life! (a toast).

lek honik, enjoy life; be well off; *lit.*, lick honey.

lekish, *n.* fool; dummy.

lekoved, *prep.* in honor of. Cf. **koved.**

lek un shmek, a quick taste; casual nibble; *lit.*, lick and sniff.

lemishhke, *n.* naive person; simpleton; milksop.

lemoshl, *adv.* for example. Cf. **moshl.**

lets, *n.* joker; clown; scoffer.

letsones, *n.* clowning; mockery.

levaye, *n.* funeral.

levone, *n.* moon.

leydigeyer, *n.* loafer; idler.

leymener goylem, dummy; *lit.*, clay golem.

lign, *n.* lie; falsehood.

ligner, *n.* liar.

limed, *n.* learning; study.

linker, *n.* leftist.

lishmo, *adv.* for its own sake.

lokh in kop, hole in the head.

loksh, *n.* **1.** *pl.* **lokshn.** noddle. **2.** *fig.* Tall, thin person.

loshn hore, evil gossip; defamation.

loshn koydesh, Hebrew; *lit.*, holy tongue. Cf. **Ivrit.**

loy aleykhem, heaven preserve you.

loy aleynu, heaven preserve us.

loy mit an alef, absolutely not.

loyt, *prep.* according to.

loz lebn, let live.

lshone toyve, happy new year.

luftmentsh, *n.* impractical dreamer; idler; *lit.*, air person.
mabl, *n.* deluge; torrent.
madreyge, *n.* level; degree.
madrikh, *n.* guide; leader.
mageyfe, *n.* plague; pestilence.
make, *n.* sore; plague; scourge.
makher, *n.* influential person; big operator; fixer; *lit.*, maker.
makherayke, *n.* contraption; gadget.
makhlaka, *n.* class; section; division. (Mod. Heb.)
makhloyke, makhloykes, *n.* quarrel.
makhsheyfe, *n.* witch (*lit.* and *fig.*).
makhshove, *n.* thought.
makh zikh nit visndik, pretend to know nothing; act unconcerned.
malekh, *n.* angel (*lit.* and *fig.*).
malekhamoves, *n.* angel of death.
malke, *n.* queen.
malpe, *n.* monkey.
mame, *n.* mother; mommy.
mame loshn, Yiddish (esp. endearing); *lit.*, mother tongue.
mamesh, *adv.* virtually; actually; literally.
mamenyu, *n.* mommy.
mamzer, *n., pl.* **mamzers, mamzeyrim. 1.** illegitimate child.
   2. rascal; rogue.
mamzerish, *adj.* roguish.
manhig, *n.* leader (as of a community).
mapole, *n.* downfall; defeat.
marshas, *n.* wicked woman.
maser, *v.* denounce; inform on.
mashke, *n.* alcoholic drink.
mashken, *n.* pawn; pledge.
be mashpie, to influence; exert influence on.
be maskim, agree; consent.
masmid, *n.* diligent student.
matone, *n.* gift.
be matriakh, to trouble; burden; impose upon.
matsev, *n.* situation; condition; status.
matseyve, *n.* gravestone.
be matsliakh, succeed; prosper.

maykhl, *n.* **1.** food; dish. **2.** treat; delicacy.

mayle, *n.* **1.** virtue; value. **2.** advantage; benefit.

mayofesnik, *n.* servile person.

mayse, *n.* **1.** story; tale. **2.** matter; affair.

mayse shehoye, true story.

mayse sotn, as luck would have it; as if to spite; *lit.*, Satan's work.

maysim toyvim, good deeds.

mazik, *n.* mischief-maker.

mazl, *n.* luck.

mazldik, *adj.* **1.** lucky. **2.** auspicious.

mazl tov, congratulations; *lit.*, good luck.

medine, *n.* country.

megile, *n.* long story.

mehalekh, *n.* long walk; long distance.

be mekane, to envy.

be mekhabed, to honor.

mekhaber, *n.* author (of a religious book).

mekhaye, *n.* delight; pleasure.

mekhaye nefoshes, delightful(ly).

mekhile, *n.* forgiveness.

mekhutn, *n., pl.* **mekhutonim.** son-in-law's or daughter-in-law's father; in-law.

mckhuteneste, *n.* son-in-law's or daughter-in-law's mother; *fem.* of **mekhutn.**

memeyle, *adv.* as a matter of course; naturally; consequently.

menahel, *n.* principal or headmaster of Jewish school (Mod. Heb.)

mentsh, *n.* decent person; good human being.

mentshlekhkayt, *n.* humaneness.

menuvl, *n.* obnoxious, contemptible person.

mes, *n., pl.* **meysim.** dead man; corpse.

be mesameyakh, celebrate; make merry.

be meshadekh, be connected by marriage (with). Cf. **shidekh.**

meshiakhs tsaytn, wondrous or miraculous occurrence; *lit.*, Messiah's times.

meshores, *n.* servant.

meshugas, *n.* madness; craze. Cf. **shigoen.**

meshuge, *adj.* crazy; insane.

meshugene(r), *n.* crazy person; lunatic.

meshugoim, *n. pl.* madmen; lunatics.

meshumed, *n.* convert (from Judaism to another religion); apostate.

mesiras nefesh, extreme devotion; self-sacrifice.

metapelet, *n.* nanny; nursemaid. (Mod. Heb.)

be metsaer, grieve; worry.

metsiye, *n.* bargain (often ironic).

metsuyon, *adj.* excellent. (Mod. Heb.)

be mevatl, disparage; belittle. Cf. **bitl.**

be mevayesh, shame; humiliate.

be mevaze, degrade.

meydl, *n.* girl.

meydele, *n.* little girl.

meylekh, *n.* king.

meylets yoysher, defender; intercessor.

meysim, *n. pl.* of **mes.**

meyvn, *n., pl.* **meyvinim.** expert; connoisseur.

mezumen, *n.* ready money; cash.

mides, *n. pl.* moral and ethical values.

mies, *adj.* ugly; loathsome; repulsive.

mieskayt, *n.* **1.** ugliness. **2.** ugly person.

milkhik, *adj.* dairy.

milkhome, *n.* war.

mime, *n.* = mume.

minestam, minhastam, *adv.* probably. Cf. **mistome.**

minheg, *n., pl.* **minhogim.** custom; ritual.

mise meshune, violent or unnatural death.

mish, *v.* mix.

mishebeyrakh, *n.* a telling off; scolding; tirade; *lit.,* a public blessing at the synagogue. Cf. **brokhe.**

mishpet, *n.* judgment.

mishpokhe, *n.* family.

mist, *n.* rubbish; garbage.

mistome, *adv.* probably. Cf. **minastam.**

mitn gantsn hartsn, wholeheartedly.

mitsve, *n.* good deed; precept; commandment.

mitun, *n.* economic slowdown. (Mod. Heb.)

mizinik, *n.* youngest son.

mizinke, *n.* youngest daughter.

moadon, *n.* club. (Mod. Heb.)

modne, *adj.* strange; odd; queer.

more, *n., fem.* **mora.** Hebrew teacher. (Mod. Heb.)

mosad, *n., pl.* **mosadot.** institute; agency. (Mod. Heb.)

moshav, *n.* Israeli cooperative village. (Mod. Heb.)

moshava, *n.* Israeli village with privately owned property. (Mod. Heb.)

moshl, *n.* example; parable. Cf. **lemoshl.**

moyd, *n.* maid; maiden; girl.

be moyde, confess.

moyekh, *n.* mind; brains.

moykhl, *interj.* no, thanks; never mind (ironic).—**be moykhl,** forgive; pardon.

moyre, *n.* fear.

moyredik, *adj.* frightful; awesome.

moyshe kapoyer, 1. contrary person. **2.** topsy-turvy. Cf. **kapoyer.** (popularized by the name of a cartoon character in a *Forverts* series by B. Kovner published in book form in 1919)

moyshef skeynim, old age home.

mume, *n.* aunt.

mumkhe, *n.* expert; specialist.

muser, *n.* reproof; moralizing.

muser haskl, moral or lesson (of a story).

mutshe, *v.* harass; torment; nag. Cf. **oysgemutshet.**

na, *interj.* here; have; take.

nakhon, *adj.* right; correct. (Mod. Heb.)

nadn, *n.* dowry.

nafke mine, difference.

nakhes, *n.* pride and joy; pleasure.

nar, *n.* fool.

narish, *adj.* foolish.

narishkayt, *n.* foolishness.

naronim, *n. pl.* fools.

nash, *v., n.* nibble; snack.

nasheray, *n.* snack foods; tidbits.

na venad, wandering; homeless.

nebekh, nebish, *interj., adj.* poor; unfortunate; pitiful.—*n.* ineffectual or unfortunate person; poor devil.

nedove, *n.* donation.

negine, *n.* Jewish music, esp. vocal. Cf. **nign.**

nekeyve, *n.* female.

nekhome, *n.* consolation.

a nekhtiker tog, nothing of the sort; *lit.*, yesterday's day.

nekome, *n.* vengeance.

nes, *n.* miracle.

neshira, *n.* process of falling off (said of immigration to Israel). Cf. **noshrim.** (Mod. Heb.)

neshome, *n.* soul.

neshomele, *n.* darling; *lit.*, little soul.

neveyle, *n.* carcass.

neveyre, *n.* = aveyre.

neyder, *n.* vow.

nifter, *n.* deceased.

nign, *n.* Jewish melody or tune. Cf. **negine.**

nishkoshe, *adv.* not bad; so-so.

nisim venifloes, miracles and wonders. Cf. **nes.**

nisoyen, *n., pl.* **nisyoynes.** temptation; ordeal.

nit do gedakht, may it never happen here; perish the thought.

nit gedayget, don't worry.

nit gefidlt, didn't succeed; failed; the deal is off.

nit haynt gedakht, may it never happen today; perish the thought.

nokh, *adv.* yet; still.

nokh a mol, once more; again.

nokhshleper, *n.* hanger-on.

noshrim, *n. pl.* Jewish immigrants to a country other than Israel; *lit.*, ones who fall off. (Mod. Heb.)

novi, *n., pl.* **neviim.** prophet.

be noyheg, be wont to; act habitually (in religious matters).

be noykem, take revenge. Cf. **nekome.**

nu, *interj.* **1.** well; so. **2.** come on; go on.

nudnik, *n.* bore; pest.

nudzh, *v.* pester; nag.—*n.* pest; nag.

nusekh, *n.* version or style (esp. of liturgy).

ofer voeyfer, dust and ashes.

okh un vey, alas; woe.

ole, *n., fem.* **ola.** immigrant to Israel; *lit.*, one who ascends. Cf. **aliya.** (Mod. Heb.)

oleho hasholem, (learned use) may she rest in peace.

olev hasholem, may he rest in peace.

olim, *n.* plural of **ole.** Cf. **khozrim, noshrim, yordim.** (Mod. Heb.)

olraytnik, *n., fem.* **olraytnitse.** upstart; parvenu. (Am. Yid. < Eng. *all right*)

onev, *n.* humble person.

ongeblozn, *adj.* puffed up; haughty; conceited.

ongeshtopt, *adj.* loaded; stuffed (as with money).

ongepatshket, *adj.* messed up; slapped together.

onshikenish, *n.* affliction; nuisance; pest.

onshtendik, *adj.* decent; respectable.

oreman, *n.* poor man; pauper.

ot, *adv.* just.

ot azoy, just so; that's it.

oves, *n. pl.* ancestors.

ovl, *n.* mourner.

oy, *interj.* oh! ouch!

oyf (or **af**) **shpilkes,** on pins and needles.

oyf (or **af**) **tsores,** in trouble.

oyf (or **af**) **tsulokhes,** for spite; spitefully.

oykh mir a, not much of a (specified person or thing).

oylem, *n.* public; audience; turnout.

oylem habe, world to come.

oylem haze, this world.

oylem hoemes, = emese velt.

oyrekh, *n., pl.* **orkhim.** visitor; guest.

oysgehaltn, *adj.* consistent.

oysgemutshet, *adj.* exhausted; worn out. Cf. **mutshe.**

oysgeputst, *adj.* dressed up; decked out in finery.

oysgeshpilt, *adj.* played out; gone to seed.

oysher, *n.* wealthy man.

oys kapelitsh makher, no more a big wheel; downgraded; *lit.*, no longer a hatmaker.

oysvorf, oysvurf, *n.* scoundrel.

oytser, *n.* treasure.

oyverbotl, *adj.* senile.

oy vey, 1. oh, dear; my goodness. **2.** = oy vey iz mir.
oy vey iz mir, woe is me.
pamelekh, *adv.* slowly.
panyebrat, *n.* close friend; chum.
parkh, parekh, *n.* scruffy, scabby person.
parnose, *n.* living; livelihood.
partsef, *n.* face; mug.
paskn, *v.* rule on a legal question; judge. Cf. **psak.**
paskudne, *adj.* nasty; mean.
paskudnyak, *n.* scoundrel; lout.
patsh, *v., n., pl.* **petsh.** slap; smack.
patshke, *v.* smear; mess around; mess up.
pavolye, *adv.* = pamelekh.
pekl, *n.* pack; bundle.
petsh, *n.* plural of **patsh.**
peyger, *v.* (of an animal) to die; also *fig.*—*n.* carcass.
pilpl, *n.* subtle, theoretical debate or argument.
pintele yid, essence of a Jew.
pips, *n.* peep; slightest sound.
pisk, *n.* mouth (vulg.); snout; grimace.
pitsl, *n.* **1.** tiny bit. **2.** little child; tot; baby.
plapl, *v.* chatter; babble.
plats, *v.* burst; explode.
pleyte, *n.* escape.
plonter, *v.* confuse; muddle.
ployder, *v.* gab; chatter.
plugte, *n.* controversy.
ponim, *n.* face.
porets, *n., pl.* **pritsim.** lord; nobleman (*lit.* and *fig.*).
poshet, *adj.* simple.
posl, *adj.* void; invalid.
poter, *adj.* exempt; rid of.
poyer, *n.* peasant; boor.
prave, *v.* celebrate; observe.
pritse, *n.* feminine of **porets.**
pritsim, *n.* plural of **porets.**
probe, *n.* tryout; rehearsal; audition.
prost, *adj.* coarse; common; plain.

prostak, *n.* coarse person.

proteksiya, *n.* influence; pull; patronage. (Mod. Heb., from Russian)

psak, *n.* legal ruling or decision.

pshore, *n.* compromise.

pupik, *n.* navel; gizzard.

pushke, *n.* charity box.

pust, *adj.* empty; forsaken.

pust un pas, idle; loafing.

raboysay, *interj.* gentlemen.

rakhmone litslan, God preserve us.

rakhmones, *n.* pity.

ram, *n.* yeshiva teacher. (acronym for Hebrew-Aramaic *reysh-metivta*)

raye, *n.* evidence; proof.

raykh vi koyrekh, very rich; *lit.*, rich as Korah (who, according to the Talmud, had amassed great wealth in Egypt).

rays shtiker, torment; *lit.*, tear pieces.

Reb, Mr.; Sir (used only with first name or full name).

reboyne shel oylem, Master of the world; Creator.

redife, *n.* persecution.

refue, *n.* cure; healing; recovery.

refue shleyme, complete recovery.

remez, *n.* (mystical) allusion; sign.

rekhiles, *n.* slander; gossip.

retekh, *n.* radish.

revakh, *n.* profit.

reyekh, *n.* smell; odor.

rikud, *n.* dance.

rirevdik, *adj.* lively; active; vivacious.

rishes, *n.* malice; evil.

riz, *n.* giant.

roshe, *n., pl.* **reshoim.** 1. evil person. 2. anti-Semite.

roshe merushe, 1. extremely evil person. 2. rabid anti-Semite.

roykh, *n.* smoke.

rozhinke, *n.* raisin.

ruekh, *n.* 1. spirit, esp. religious spirit or atmosphere. 2. ghost; demon; devil (chiefly in curses).

ruekh hakoydesh, divine spirit; inspiration.
rukhes, *n.* plural of **ruekh** (def. 2).
rukhnies, *n.* spirituality. Cf. **gashmies.**
sabra, *n.* native of Israel. (Mod. Heb.)
sakh hakl, sum total.
sakone, *n.* danger.
sakones nefoshes, extreme danger.
sam, *n.* poison.
sava, *n.* grandfather. (Mod. Heb.)
savta, *n.* grandmother. (Mod. Heb.)
say vi say, anyhow; in any case.
seyfer, *n., pl.* **sforim.** Jewish religious book.
seykhl, *n.* intelligence; common sense.
sgule, *n.* remedy; safeguard.
sha, *interj.* hush; quiet.
Shabaton, *n., pl.* **Shabatons, Shabatonim.** Sabbath social
    gathering. (Mod. Heb.)
shadkhn, *n.* matchmaker.
shalom, *n.* **1.** hello or good-bye. **2.** peace. (Mod. Heb.)
shames, *n., pl.* **shamosim. 1.** beadle. **2.** assistant.
shande, *n.* shame.
shavua tov, = gut vokh. (Mod. Heb.)
shayekh, *adj.* pertinent; relevant.
shaykhes, *n.* connection; bearing; relevance.
shayle, *n.* question, esp. on a religious matter.
shed, *n., pl.* **sheydim.** ghost; demon.
sheker, *n.* falsehood.
sheket, *n., interj.* silence; quiet. (Mod. Heb.)
skekoyekh, *interj.* = yasher koyekh.
sheliyakh, *n.* representative; delegate; emissary.
shemevdik, *adj.* shy; bashful.
sherut, *n.* taxi service in Israel. (Mod. Heb.)
sheygets, *n., pl.* **shkotsim. 1.** young non-Jew. **2.** sinful young Jew.
    3. roguish fellow.
sheyn, *adj.* beautiful; handsome; fair.
sheynkayt, *n.* beauty; a beauty.
shidekh, *n.* marital match. (also *fig.*).
shier, *n.* **1.** limit. **2.** lesson.

shigoen, *n.* madness; whim. Cf. **meshugas.**

shiker, *adj.* drunk.—*n.* drunkard.

shikse, *n.* non-Jewish woman, esp. a young woman.

shikun, *n.* housing block or project in Israel. (Mod. Heb.)

shikyingl, *n.* errand boy.

shirayim, *n. pl.* leftovers.

shkheynes, *n.* vicinity. Cf. **shokhn.**

shkie, *n.* sunset.

shkotsim, *n.* plural of **sheygets.**

shlak, *n.* **1.** stroke. **2.** nuisance. **3.** junk.

shlekht, *adj.* bad.

shlemazl, *n.* **1.** unlucky person; ne'er-do-well. **2.** bad luck; misfortune.

shlemiel, shlemil, *n.* clumsy, bungling person; simpleton; fool.

shlep, *v., n.* drag (*lit.* and *fig.*).

shleper, *n.* tramp; bum.

shlof, *v., n.* sleep.

shlog, *v.* stroke; hit; beat.

shlog al khet, say mea culpa; admit guilt; repent; *lit.*, beat (one's chest in reciting) the confession on the Day of Atonement.

shlump, *n.* sloppy, dowdy person.—*v.* drag; bedraggle.

shlumperdik, *adj.* sloppy; dowdy.

shm-, prefix used to reduplicate a word in deprecation, as *fancy-shmancy, old-shmold.*

shmad, *n.* conversion from Judaism. Cf. **geshmat, meshumed.**

shmaltsgrub, *n.* goldmine; jackpot; *lit.*, fat mine.

shmate, *n.* rag (*lit.* and *fig.*).

shmay, *v.* bustle; be busy.

shmek tabik, 1. pinch of snuff. **2.** *fig.* worthless thing.

shmendrik, *n.* ineffectual or insignificant person; nonentity; fool. (from *Shmendrik,* name of a character in an operetta by Abraham Goldfaden, 1840–1908)

shmerl, *n.* anybody; every Tom, Dick, and Harry.

shmigege, *n.* silly or stupid person; simpleton; nitwit.

shmo, *n.* = shmigege. (short for Yid. *shmok,* a vulgarism)

shmontses, *n.* nonsense.

shmus, shmues, *n.* conversation; discussion; chat.

shmuts, *n.* dirt; smut.

shmutsik, *n.* dirty; foul.
shnaps, *n.* whiskey.
shnorer, *n.* beggar.
shnuk, *n.* fool; *lit.,* (elephant) trunk, snout.
shnur, shnir, *n.* daughter-in-law.
shoa, *n.* holocaust; *Yom Hashoa,* Holocaust Memorial Day. (Mod. Heb.)
shokher, *n. pl.* **shkhoyrim.** black (man).
shokhn, *n., pl.* **shkheynim.** neighbor.
shokl, *v.* shake; sway (esp. in prayer).
sholem, *n.* **1.** peace. **2.** hello. Cf. **shalom.**
sholem aleykhem, peace unto you (greeting).
sholem bayis, household bliss; harmony between mates.
shoyn, *adv.* already.
shoyte, *n.* fool.
shpas, *n.* joke; gag.
shpatsir, *v., n.* stroll; walk.
shpay, *v.* spit.
shpilkes, *n. pl.* jitters; *lit.,* pins.
shpits, *n.* tip.
shprits, *v., n.* squirt; soda drink.
shray khay vekayem, to protest in vain; *lit.,* shout 'living and eternal (God).'
shreklekh, *adj.* terrible; awful.
shtark, *adj.* strong.
shtarker, *n.* strong man; stout fellow.
shtele, *n.* job; position.
shtetl, *n.* town with a Jewish community in eastern Europe.
shtifer, *n.* mischievous child; brat; practical joker.
shtiferay, *n.* mischief; pranks.
shtik, *n.* **1.** act; routine; prank; gimmick. **2.** bit; piece.
shtikl, *n. pl.* **shtiklekh.** bit; piece.
shtolts, *adj.* proud; conceited.
shtoltser, *n.* conceited person; show-off.
shtoltsir, *v.* take pride in; show off.
shtup, *v., n.* push; shove.
shtus, *n.* folly; nonsense.
shuk, *n.* large outdoor market in Israel; *lit.,* street; market. (Mod. Heb.)

shul, *n.* synagogue.

shule, *n.* secular (Yiddishist) school.

shutef, *n.* partner.

shutfes, *n.* partnership.

shvakh, *adj.* weak.

shvartse(r), *n.* black person.

shvarts yor, devil; hell; *lit.*, black year.

shvegerin, *n.* sister-in-law.

¹shver, *n.* father-in-law.

²shver, *adj.* heavy; difficult.

shviger, *n.* mother-in-law.

shvindl, *n.* swindle.

shvits, shvitsbod, *n.* Turkish bath.

shvitser, *n.* **1.** overaggressive, push y person. **2.** hard worker; workaholic. **3.** (*lit.*) one who sweats.

shvoger, *n.* brother-in-law.

shvue, *n.* oath.

sibe, *n.* cause; reason.

sikha, *n., pl.* **sikhot.** discussion. (Mod. Heb.)

simen, *n.* sign.

simkhe, *n.* **1.** happy occasion; party; celebration. **2.** joy.

sine, *n.* hatred; hate.

skhar, *n.* reward.

skhoyre, *n.* merchandise; goods.

skotsl kumt, look who's here; welcome.

slikha, *n., interj.* pardon. (Mod. Heb.)

smakh, *n.* basis; ground; authority.

smetene, *n.* sour cream.

snif, *n.* branch; division. (Mod. Heb.)

sod, *n.* secret.

sof, *n.* end.

sofek, *n.* doubt.

sotn, *n.* devil; Satan.

soyfer, *n.* scribe.

soykher, *n., pl.* **sokhrim.** merchant; businessman.

soyne, *n.* enemy.

stam, *adv.* no more than; only; merely; just.

stam azoy, just like that; without reason.

staytsh, *interj.* how come; how is it possible.
strashe, *v.* threaten.
sude, *n.* festive meal; banquet.
svive, *n.* environment; surroundings.
svore, *n.* guess; conjecture; hypothesis.
taam, *n.* = tam (taste).
take, *adv.* indeed; really.
takhles, *n.* practical purpose; goal.
takhrikhim, *n. pl.* burial shrouds.
takhshet, *n.* brat. (Yid. < Heb. *takhshit* jewel, adornment)
talmid, *n.* disciple; student.
¹**tam,** *n.* taste; good taste.
²**tam,** *n.* simple, naive person; simpleton.
tamevate, *adj.* simple-minded; foolish. —*n.* simpleton.
tam gan eydn, delicious taste; *lit.*, taste of paradise.
tamtses, *n.* essence; gist.
tante, *n.* aunt.
tap, *v.* touch; feel by touch.
tararam, *n.* fuss; to-do.
tate, *n.* father; dad.
tate-mame, *n.* parents.
tatenyu, *n.* dear father; daddy.
tayne, *n.* claim; complaint.
tayneg, *n.* pleasure; delight.
taytsh, *n.* meaning; explanation.
tenua, *n.* (political or social) movement. (Mod. Heb.)
terets, *n., pl.* **terutsim. 1.** reply; response. **2.** pretext; excuse.
teuda, *n.* diploma. (Mod. Heb.)
teudat ole, certificate of immigration to Israel. (Mod. Heb.)
teykef, *adj.* instantly; at once.
teykef umiyad, immediately; directly.
tfile, *n.* prayer.
tfise, *n.* prison.
tirkhe, *n.* pains; effort; burden.
tish, *n.* table.
tishtekh, *n.* tablecloth.
tiskhadesh, *interj.* wear it in good health. (Yid. < Heb., may you renew yourself)

tiyul, *n.* long walk; hike. (Mod. Heb.)
tlie, *n.* gallows.
tochnit, *n.* program. (Mod. Heb.)
toda, *interj., n.* thanks (Mod. Heb.)
toda raba, many thanks. (Mod. Heb.)
toes, *n.* mistake.
tokhes, *n.* backside.
tomid, *adv.* always; ever.
tones, *n., pl.* **taneysim.** fast; fast day.
be toye, make a mistake.
toyg, *v.* be good for; qualify.
toyg af kapores, be good for nothing; be useless; *lit.*, be fit for a scapegoat on Yom Kippur.
toykhekhe, *n.* heap of curses; series of calamities.
toyve, *n.* favor.
treyf, *adj.* not kosher; illegal; illegitimate.
trombenik, *n.* **1.** braggart; bluffer. **2.** freeloader.
tsadik, *n.* righteous person.
tsar, *n.* grief; sorrow.
tsar bale khayim, pity for living creatures.
tsatske, *n.* **1.** toy; trinket; gadget. **2.** *fig.* brat.
tsavoe, *n.* last will.
tsdoke, *n.* charity.
tseylem, *n.* cross; crucifix.
tshatshke, *n.* = tsatske.
tshep, *v.* pick on; pester.
tshuve, *n.* **1.** penitence. **2.** response.
tsibele, *n.* onion.
tsigayner, *n.* gypsy.
tsimes, *n.* **1.** fruit or vegetable stew. **2.** *fig.* big deal; fuss; to-do.
tsiter, *v.* tremble.
tsnies, *n.* modesty.
tsore, tsure, *n.* trouble; calamity.
tsores, tsures, *n. pl.* troubles; problems; aggravation.
tsudreyt, *adj.* confused; mixed up; unhinged.
tsudreyter, *n.* mixed-up person.
tsu gezunt, to health; bless you (after a sneeze, etc.).
tsu got un tsu layt, perfect in every way; *lit.*, to God and to people.

tsukrokhn, *adj.* uncouth; ungainly.

tsumisht, *adj.* mixed up.

tsulokhes, *n.* spite.

tsutumlt, *n.* confused; dazed.

tsutshepenish, *n.* nuisance; pest; (*lit.* and *fig.*) parasite.

tsutsik, *n.* puppy; colt.

tuml, *n.* commotion; racket; noise.

tumler, *n.* life of the party; master of ceremonies; *lit.*, noisemaker.

ulpan, *n.* Hebrew language class or course (Mod. Heb.)

umgelumpert, *adj.* awkward; clumsy.

unterfirer, *n.* best man.

untershte shure, bottom line.

vaad, *n.* board; council.

valger, *v.* roll around; wander; roam.

vants, *n.* bedbug.

vayivrakh, *n.* escape; flight.

vayter, *adv.* further; next.

vehoraye, *conj.* and here's the proof. Cf. **raye.**

velt, *n.* world.

ver veyst, who knows.

vesh, *n.* wash; laundry.

vider amol, once again; over again.

vikhtik, *adj.* important.

vikuakh, *n.* debate; disputation.

vits, *n.* joke.

vokhedik, *adj.* everyday; workaday; commonplace.

vontses, *n. pl.* mustaches.

vort, *n.* **1.** word. **2.** saying; discourse. **3.** pledge; promise.

vos tut zikh, how are things; what's new.

vu den, sure; certainly; what else would you expect.

yahadut, *n.* Judaism; Jewishness. (Mod. Heb.)

yakhne, *n.* female meddler or busybody.

yakhsn, *n.* one who claims status or pedigree; privileged person (often ironic). Cf. **yikhes.**

yakres, *n.* dearth; scarcity.

yarid, *n.* **1.** fair. **2.** *fig.* uproar.

yarshn, *v.* inherit.

yasher koyekh, 1. expression of appreciation; thanks. **2.** well done; more power to you! Also, **shekoyekh.**

yemakh shmoy, may his name be blotted out.

yene velt, next world; hereafter.

yente, *n.* female busybody; gossipy woman (also transf. to males).

yerida, *n.* emigration of Jews from Israel. Cf. **yordim.** (Mod. Heb.)

yerushe, *n.* inheritance; heritage.

yeshue, *n.* salvation.

yesod, *n.* basis; groundwork.

yesurim, *n. pl.* aches and pains; torments.

yeytser hore, 1. evil inclination. **2.** temptation; lust.

yid, *n., pl.* **yidn.** Jew.

yidene, *n., fem.* of **yid. 1.** Jewish woman, esp. matron. **2.** (humorous) one's wife.

yidishkayt, *n.* Judaism; Jewishness.

yikhes, *n.* **1.** distinguished ancestry; pedigree. **2.** status; privilege.

yingatsh, *n.* = yungatsh.

yingl, *n.* boy.

yingele, *n.* little boy.

yires shomayim, 1. fear of God. **2.** God-fearing person.

yhisuv, *n.* **1.** (Jewish) settlement (in Israel). **2.** community.

yofi, *interj.* very good; excellent. (Mod. Heb.)

yogenish, *n.* rush; hurry; haste.

yold, *n.* dupe; fool.

yontev, *n.* holiday.

yontevdik, *adj.* festive.

yordim, *n. pl.* Jewish emigrants from Israel; *lit.,* those who descend. Cf. **khozrim, noshrim, olim.** (Mod. Heb.)

yortsayt, *n.* anniversary of death.

yosem, *n., fem.* **yesoyme;** *pl.* **yesoymim.** orphan.

yoykh, *n.* **1.** broth, esp. rich broth. **2.** chicken soup.

yoyresh, *n., pl.* **yorshim.** heir.

yoysher, *n.* justice; fairness.

be yoytse, do one's duty.

yung, *n.* fellow; youth; lad.

yungatsh, *n.* brat; rascal.

yungelayt, *n. pl.* young men.

yungvarg, *n.* young people; youth.

zaftik, *adj.* **1.** juicy; luscious. **2.** *fig.* plump; buxom.
zay azoy gut, please; *lit.*, be so good.
zay gezunt, good-bye; be well.
zemer, *n.* Jewish song or tune.
zets, *n.* punch; bump; slam.
zeyde, *n.* grandfather.
zhlob, *n.* gross person; oaf.
zifts, *n.* sigh.
zikhroyne livrokhe, of blessed memory.
zikorn, *n.* memory.
zis, *adj.* sweet.
ziskayt, *n.* sweetness (esp. *fig.*).
zivig, *n.* destined match or mate. Cf. **basherte(r).**
zkhus, *n.* privilege; merit; religious deserts.
zkhus oves, ancestral merit.
zman, *n.* school semester; *lit.*, time.
zmires, *n. pl.* Sabbath songs.
zog gornit, say nothing.
zokn, *n., pl.* **zkeynim.** old man.
zol zayn azoy, so be it.
zorg zikh nisht, don't worry.
be zoykhe, be worthy; have the privilege to; live to see.

Notes

Introduction

1. "Borrowing" is the traditional term in historical and comparative linguistics for the transfer of a word or other element from one language to another. The concept of borrowing was refined by Uriel Weinreich and Einar Haugen to include the process of *interference* (deviations introduced by bilinguals into one language under the influence of another), which occurs in the course of continuous *switching* from one language to another, and which ultimately results in the *integration* of an interfering element into one or the other of the two languages.

2. Leonard Bloomfield, *Language* (New York: Henry Holt, 1933), p. 461.

3. Ibid. Contemporary linguists would probably use "dominant" and "nondominant" or "majority language" and "minority language" in place of "upper" and "lower." Other euphemistic usages are cited by Haugen, "Bilingualism, Language Contact, and Immigrant Languages in the United States," p. 513.

4. The Yiddish and Yiddish-origin words in this book are transcribed in the standard romanization system of the YIVO Institute for Jewish Research (formerly the American National Standard Romanization of Yiddish), with the following two exceptions: (1) When a Yiddish-origin word appears in an English citation, the actual spelling used in the citation is retained; (2) when the spelling of the Yiddish-origin word or name has become standardized in

English or in another language (as the word *Yiddish* itself or the name *Sholom Aleichem*, which in the YIVO system are rendered *yidish* and *Sholem aleykhem*), the standard English (Dutch, etc.) spelling is retained. English words borrowed from Modern Hebrew are transcribed in a modified version of the American National Standard for the Romanization of Hebrew. For more details see Appendix I: "The Romanization of Yiddish and Yiddish-Origin Words."

5. It is significant that most Yiddish loans that have become popular in English appear in standard dictionaries with the label *Slang*. There are, however, inconsistencies in the labeling, as pointed out in my article, "The Labeling of Yiddish- and Hebrew-Origin Lexemes in Several English Dictionaries," *Jewish Language Review* 2 (1982): 34–39.

6. A comprehensive linguistic study of Yiddish-English contact has often been called for, but apparently a great deal of preparatory fieldwork needs to be done before such a study becomes feasible. The standard sociolinguistic work in the field is Joshua A. Fishman, *Yiddish in America: Sociolinguistic Description and Analysis. International Journal of American Linguistics,* vol. 31, No. 2 (Indiana University Press, 1965).

Chapter 1

1. H. L. Mencken, *The American Language* (New York: Alfred A. Knopf, 4th ed., 1936), pp. 216–17. Similar descriptions appear in the earlier editions, the first of which was published in 1919.

2. Rosten defined Yinglish as "Yiddish words that are used in colloquial English in both the United States and the United Kingdom: *kibitzer, mish-mash, bagel,* etc." (*The Joys of Yiddish,* Pocket Book ed., 1970, p. ix). The term has long been used in the sense of "a Yiddish-English mixture": see for example H. J. Gans, "The 'Yinglish' Music of Mickey Katz," *American Quarterly* 21 (1953): 442–50, 555–63, and Rose Nash, "Spanglish: Language Contact in Puerto Rico," *American Speech* 45 (1974): 223–33, in which reference is made to certain "well-known language mixtures, such as Franglais, Yinglish, Japlish" (p. 224).

3. Stuart Berg Flexner, "Preface to the Supplement," *Dictionary*

of American Slang (New York: Thomas Y. Crowell, 1960, Supplemented ed., 1967), p. 670.

4. Clarence L. Barnhart, "On Matters Lexicographical," *American Speech* 45 (1973): 106–7.

5. A scathing review of this book was given by David L. Gold, *American Speech* 59 (1984): 172–75.

6. H. Beem, "Yiddish in Holland," *The Field of Yiddish,* ed. U. Weinreich (New York: Linguistic Circle of New York, 1954), p. 133.

7. The spread and distribution of Yiddishisms in the United States is being recorded in the *Dictionary of American Regional English* (DARE), a major study of English as spoken in 1,002 communities across the United States, in progress since 1965 under the direction of Frederic G. Cassidy at the University of Wisconsin. See for example the entry *farblonjet* cited by Joan H. Hall, "DARE: The View from the Letter F," *Dictionaries* 1 (1979): 25–46.

8. See Lillian Mermin Feinsilver, "Like Influences from Yiddish and Pennsylvania German," *American Speech* 33 (1958): 231–33.

9. According to the *American Jewish Yearbook* of 1991 (Philadelphia: The Jewish Publication Society of America, 1991), the Jewish population of the United States stood in 1990 at approximately 5.981 million, with about 1,700,000 Jews located in the New York City metropolitan area. The total world Jewish population in 1990 was approximately thirteen million.

Chapter 2

1. According to Gold, *Jewish Language Review* 1, p. 19. "The linguistic term *Jewish language* . . . probably goes back no further than the 1920s or 1930s." In 1979, Gold, Leonard Prager, and others founded the Association for the Study of Jewish Languages, which publishes the annual *Jewish Language Review,* a publication devoted to all linguistic matters of Jewish interest but principally to the investigation of Jewish languages, including present-day varieties such as Modern Judezmo, Modern Ebri, Modern Karaitic, and Modern Bukharic. The *Encyclopaedia Judaica* has an article on Jewish Languages (vol. 10, 1972) by Solomon A. Birnbaum, as well as individual articles under such conventional headings as "Judeo-Arabic,"

"Judeo-French," etc. For a discussion of Jewish languages from a sociolinguistic standpoint, see J. A. Fishman, "The Sociology of Jewish Languages from the Perspective of the General Sociology of Language" (1981).

2. The decimation of European Jewry in the Holocaust reduced drastically the number of Yiddish speakers. In 1980, the total estimated number of Yiddish speakers in the world was 3,663,420 (compiled from statistical data supplied by Dina Abramowicz, librarian of the YIVO Institute for Jewish Research). Some have placed the number closer to five million.

3. The periodization scheme of Yiddish shown here is that given by Max Weinreich, "Prehistory and Early History of Yiddish" (p. 91, note 43), and by Uriel Weinreich, "Yiddish Language," (p. 795). Other schemes have been proposed, as that of Süsskind (1953) and Joffe (1943).

4. Rashi (1040–1105) in his commentaries frequently explains words by giving their German equivalents as glosses, calling them *leshon 'ashkenaz*. Max Weinreich points out in his *History of the Yiddish Language* (Chicago: The University of Chicago Press, 1980), p. 6, that "Disregarding the fact that Rashi's commentary came down to us in relatively late copies, it is nevertheless worth mentioning that several Yiddish glosses are found in Rashi, that is, dating from ca. 1100."

5. The Hebrew word *loez* originally meant a foreign language (Psalms 114:1). In early medieval times it became identified with Latin and the Romance languages into which Latin evolved, especially Old Italian and Old French. A variant form, *laaz* (plural *leazim*), came to mean a foreign gloss rendered in Hebrew letters. Since most of the medieval rabbinical glosses were from Romance languages, the formula *belaaz* eventually acquired the meaning 'in Old French' due to the fact that most of Rashi's 4,800 glosses on the Bible and Talmud were renderings of Old French words (forming incidentally a most valuable source for the study of the earliest stage of the French language).

6. The negative sense of Yiddish *yente* (also spelled *yenta* in American English slang) apparently derives from the name of a gossipy comic character, *Yente Telebende,* in the writings of the

Yiddish humorist B. Kovner (pseudonym of Jacob Adler), which appeared in the 1920s and 1930s in the *Jewish Daily Forward*. (See also *moyshe kapoyer* in the Glossary, Appendix II). Similarly, the synonymous *yakhne*, which derives ultimately from Hebrew *Yocheved*, was influenced in meaning by *Di Bobe Yakhne*, a wicked witch in a play by Abraham Goldfaden, 1840–1908. Some other common Yiddish names of Romance origin are *Shprintse* (from Jewish Italian *Speranza*) and *Fayvish* (ultimately from Latin *Phoebus*).

7. M. Weinreich, *History of the Yiddish Language*, p. 397.

8. U. Weinreich, "Yiddish Language," p. 792.

Chapter 3

1. My sources for these and other population statistics are Raphael Patai, *Tents of Jacob: The Diaspora—Yesterday and Today* (New Jersey: Prentice-Hall, 1971), pp. 334, 361, and Abram L. Sachar, *A History of the Jews* (New York: Alfred A. Knopf, 1953), p. 302 ff.

2. Stanley Feldstein, *The Land That I Show You: Three Centuries of Jewish Life in America* (New York: Anchor Books, 1979), p. 125.

3. Alistair Cook, "America—The Huddled Masses," *The Listener* (January 18, 1973): 78.

4. Peter Farb, *Word Play* (New York: Alfred A. Knopf, 1974), p. 163.

5. J. A. Fishman, *Yiddish in America*, p. 41.

6. Leo Wiener, *The History of Yiddish Literature in the Nineteenth Century* (London: John C. Nimmo, 1899, now reprinted), p. 11.

7. These statistics were obtained from the YIVO Institute for Jewish Research. *The World Jewish Press*, published by the World Jewish Congress, and *The American Jewish Yearbook*, both of 1983, together list over a hundred Yiddish magazines and journals published worldwide.

8. There are Yiddish departments at the Hebrew University in Jerusalem, Bar-Ilan University in Ramat Gan, and the University of Haifa. The 1982 volume of *Yidishe shprakh* was devoted to the theme of Yiddish in Israel, with articles such as "Five Hundred Years of Yiddish in Israel" by Mordkhe Schaechter, and "Yiddish Sports

Terminology in the Israeli Press," by Itsik Gotesman. See also Joshua A. and David. E. Fishman, "Yiddish in Israel: The Press, Radio, Theatre, and Book Publishing," *YIDDISH* 1 (1973): 4–23.

9. For statistics indicating the permanent character of Jewish immigration into the United States, see R. Patai, *Tents of Jacob,* p. 360. "Following the introduction of immigration quotas in 1924," writes Patai, "the flow of immigration was reduced but did not stop; nor did it stop during World War I, the depression years, World War II, or following the establishment of Israel." In the years 1933–41, 158,000 Jewish immigrants entered the country; in 1944–59, 196,693; and in 1960–68, 73,000. The end of the Cold War witnessed a renewed Russian Jewish immigration as well as an increase in Israeli immigration to the United States.

10. Joseph C. Landis, "Yiddish is Alive and Well," p. 5. See also J. A. Fishman, *Yiddish in America,* pp. 48–51.

11. See Gloria Donen Sosin, "Yiddish *Lebt Takeh* (Lives Indeed) in Westchester," *The New York Times,* August 5, 1979 (Westchester section, p. 17), where Westchester County, New York *shules* are listed along with other local institutions where Yiddish is taught.

12. Uriel Weinreich, *Languages in Contact,* p. 106.

13. J. A. Fishman, *Yiddish in America,* p. 73.

14. *Mendele* was named after the fictional character Mendele Moykher-Sforim, "Mendele the bookseller," made famous by Sholem-Yankev Abramovitsh (1836–1917), the founding father of modern Yiddish literature.

15. H. L. Mencken, *The American Language,* 4th ed. (1936), p. 633. The passage in which this information appears is worth citing in full:

> At the Census of 1930, 1,222,658 Jews gave Yiddish as their mother-tongue; in all probability another million could then speak it, or, at all events, understand it. Since the cutting off of immigration from Eastern Europe it has been declining, and there are many Jews who view it hostilely as a barbaric jargon, and hope to see it extirpated altogether; nevertheless, there are still thirty-seven Yiddish periodicals in the country, including twelve daily newspapers, and one of the latter, the Jewish *Daily Forward* of New York, had a circulation of 125,000 in 1935.

16. Compare J. A. Fishman, [On Yiddish, Modernization, and Re-ethnification], *Afn shvel* (1982): 1–7.

17. J. A. Fishman, [On The Future of Yiddish], *Afn shvel* (1983): 2–4.

Chapter 4

1. Shmuel Niger, [On Admitting Anglicisms], *Yidishe shprakh* 1 (1941): 21 (translated from Yiddish). From 1891 to 1928 Alexander Harkavy compiled a series of English-Yiddish and Yiddish-English dictionaries that were standard reference books among Yiddish speakers for over fifty years.

2. Max Weinreich, [On English Elements in Standard Yiddish], *Yidishe shprakh* 1 (1941): 33–46.

3. Judah A. Joffe, "The Development of Yiddish in the United States," *Universal Jewish Encyclopedia* 10 (1943): 601f.

4. Much has been written about American Yiddish, especially in the pages of *Yidishe shprakh*. See also J. A. Joffe (1943), which summarizes this variety of Yiddish; U. Weinreich (1949, 1953), which contain many examples of American Yiddish usage; G. Wolfe, "Notes on American Yiddish," *American Mercury* 29 (1933): 473–79; J. H. Neumann, "Notes on American Yiddish," *Journal of English and Germanic Philology* 37 (1938): 403–21; H. B. Wells, "Notes on Yiddish," *American Speech* 4 (1928): 58–66; Lawrence M. Davis, "The Stressed Vowels of Yiddish-American English," *Publication of American Dialect Society,* 48 (1967): 51–59; and Joan R. Rayfield, "The Languages of a Bilingual Community," *Janua Linguarum,* Series Practica 77 (The Hague: Mouton Co., 1970).

5. A valuable reference to early borrowings from American English is Abraham Cahan's glossary appended to the second volume of his *Bleter fun mayn lebn* (a five-volume autobiography published in 1926–31). The glossary includes and defines in Yiddish such useful new words as *overtaym* ('overtime,' defined by Cahan as "more working hours than the usual working day"), *fonograf* ("gramophone"), *sveting-sheper* ("miserable workingplaces"), *sveter* ("proprietor of a miserable workingplace; he who causes another to sweat"), and *mises* ("landlady; partly as a joke it means also a wife:

'his mises'—his wife"). There are about four hundred terms listed in the glossary.

6. Uriel Weinreich, *Modern English-Yiddish Yiddish-English Dictionary,* YIVO Institute for Jewish Research (New York: McGraw-Hill Book Co., 1968).

7. This generally tallies with the conclusions of a similar study made by Joan R. Rayfield, "The Languages of a Bilingual Community," who writes (p. 58): "A sample count from *Forverts* . . . gives about ten per cent of English words, of which only a small fraction, perhaps one-fifth, is necessary in the sense that there is no convenient Yiddish equivalent."

8. U. Weinreich, *Languages in Contact,* p. 56.

9. This plural was formed by analogy with such Yiddish forms as *lokh* 'hole,' plural *lekher, dorf* 'village,' plural *derfer.*

10. This is the Yiddish suppletive plural for words ending in –*man*; e.g., *yungeman* 'young man,' plural *yungelayt, landsman* 'countryman,' plural *landslayt.*

11. Borrowed in turn by American English as *allrightnik*: "It was, to use a term favored by the intellectuals of the fifties, the allrightniks who did the most expensive traveling" (Jason Epstein, quoted in *The New York Times Magazine,* March 26, 1972, p. 108).

12. Maurice Samuel, *In Praise of Yiddish,* pp. 270–73.

13. Yudel Mark, [On Yiddish Anglicisms], *Yorbukh fun Amopteyl fun Yivo* 1 (1938): 296–321.

14. The word appeared in a translation of a story by I. B. Singer: "After a while I was bringing my paycheck—the *paydy,* they called it in our Americanized Yiddish—to Libby" (Isaac Bashevis Singer, "Property," *New Yorker,* December 9, 1972, p. 41).

15. Solomon Poll, "The Role of Yiddish in American Ultra-Orthodox and Hasidic Communities," *YIVO Annual of Jewish Social Science* 13 (1965): 135. "Notwithstanding the fact," writes Poll, "that Yiddish is the daily spoken language of the ultrareligious groups in America, English has penetrated deeply even into the most religious groups. Many English words have been incorporated into the Yiddish vocabulary of all but the most puristically inclined" (p. 142). See also George Jochnowitz, "Bilingualism and Dialect Mixture Among Lubavitcher Hasidic Children," pp. 193–94.

Chapter 5

1. The dates of earliest recorded appearance shown here and below are from the *Oxford English Dictionary* (OED) or its Supplement, Harold Wentworth and Stuart B. Flexner, *Dictionary of American Slang* (New York: Thomas Y. Crowell, 1960, Supplemented ed., 1967), and the files of Clarence L. Barnhart, Inc. The Yiddish-origin words are transcribed in the YIVO system of Romanization of Yiddish (see Introduction, note 4).

2. Morris U. Schappes, ed., *A Documentary History of the Jews of the United States, 1654–1875* (New York: The Citadel Press, 1950), p. 113.

3. Stanley Feldstein, *The Land That I Show You: Three Centuries of Jewish Life in America* (New York: Anchor Books, 1979), p. 7.

4. Eric Partridge, *A Dictionary of the Underworld* (New York: Macmillan Co., 1950), p. 298.

5. For more on this word, see L. M. Feinsilver, "Yiddish *Ganef*: Its Family and Friends," p. 147.

6. David W. Maurer, "Underworld Etymologies: Series Three," *American Speech* 21 (1946): 69; Gerald L. Cohen, "A Shortcoming of English Dictionaries: Their Etymological Treatment of Yiddish-Origin Lexemes," paper read at the Second International Conference on General and Jewish Lexicography, University of Delaware, August 1980.

7. For more on Yiddishisms in underworld slang, see David L. Gold's review of *Whiz Mob* (1964), by David W. Maurer, in *Jewish Language Review* 2 (1982): 137–39.

8. H. L. Mencken, *The American Language,* 4th edition and two Supplements, with annotations and new material by Raven I. McDavid, Jr., with the assistance of David W. Maurer (New York: Alfred A. Knopf, 1963), pp. 259–62.

9. J. Redding Ware, *Passing English* (London: George Routledge & Sons, 1905, reprint 1972), p. v.

10. Cahan wrote *The Imported Bridegroom and Other Stories of the New York Ghetto* (1898), *Yekl* (1899), which was turned in the 1970s into the film *Hester Street,* and *The White Terror and the Red* (1905).

11. For the etymological steps by which Yiddish *mezumen* became English *mezuma*, see David L. Gold, "Etymology of English Slang *Mazuma*," *Comments on Etymology* 12 (1982): 29–30.

12. An elaboration on the OED's allusion to the Talmud is found in Nathan Süsskind, "*Origin of Shlmeil*," *Comments on Etymology* 9 (1980): 2, reprinted from Robert M. Copeland and Nathan Süsskind, eds., *The Language of Herz's "Esther": A Study of Judeo-German Dialectology* (University: The University of Alabama Press, 1976), pp. 167–74. Briefly, according to Süsskind's account the transformation of the name of Shelumiel ben Zurishaddai, the chief of the tribe of Simeon, to the designation of a classic bungler is rooted in the identification of Shelumiel in the Talmud (*Sanhedrin* 82b) with Zimri ben Salu, the Simeonite prince who was killed by Phinehas while fornicating with a Midianite woman (Numbers 25:6–15; see the commentary of Bal Haturim on Numbers 1:16 and 25:12). Zimri's predicament, which is embellished in the Talmud and Midrash, was taken as a morbidly humorous instance of a supremely luckless fellow; but since a direct reference to Zimri might stir lascivious thoughts, pious scholars took to using the name of Shelumiel, the chief prince of the Simeonites, as a veiled reference to the Simeonite prince Zimri. Implied in this "private joke of pious scholars," as Süsskind describes it, is the additional irony of Shelumiel's lucklessness in having become—quite innocently—a substitute for the lecherous Zimri. See also Arthur Norman, "The Schlemihl Problem," *American Speech* 28 (1952): 149–50.

13. "Miscellany," *American Speech* 4 (1928): 159.

14. David W. Maurer, *Language of the Underworld* (Lexington: The University of Kentucky Press, 1981), pp. 129, 251.

15. Hyman E. Goldin, *Dictionary of American Underworld Lingo* (New York: Twayne Publishers, 1950), p. 190.

16. The spelling *sch* for *sh* (frequently and regrettably found for dozens of loanwords from Yiddish) goes back to a misleading convention of transcribing Yiddish-origin words as though they derived from German. The Yiddish word *borsht* is Slavic in origin; the Yiddish word *shlemiel* is Hebrew in origin; the German spelling *sch* should have no truck with either word, nor with any word in *sh*-derived from Yiddish (e.g., *shmo, fancy-shmancy, money-shmoney*).

17. H. L. Mencken, *The American Language,* Supplement II (New York: Alfred A. Knopf, 1948), p. 754.

18. See David L. Gold, "The English Reflexes of the Yiddish Verb *Shmuesn/Shmusn,*" *Comments on Etymology* 12 (1983): 21.

19. H. L. Mencken, *The American Language* (1948), p. 757.

20. Ibid., p. 771.

21. L. M. Feinsilver, *The Taste of Yiddish,* pp. 332–33; David L. Gold, "Three English Words of Jewish Interest That Need More Study: *Shmoo, Borax,* and *Schlock,*" *Comments on Etymology* 12 (1982): 11–13.

22. H. L. Mencken, *The American Language* (1948), p. 753.

23. I owe the derivation of *dokus* to David Gold, "Etymological Studies of Jewish Interest, Part I," *Comments on Etymology* 12 (1982): 48. For a fuller discussion of this word, see L. M. Feinsilver, "Yiddish Idioms in American English," *American Speech* 37 (1962): 205, note 42, and her more recent "Yiddish for Fun and Profit," *Verbatim* 10 (1983): 1.

24. Julius G. Rothenberg, "Some American Idioms from the Yiddish," *American Speech* 18 (1943): 43–48.

25. Donn O'Meara, "American-Jewish Alphabetical Expressions," *American Speech* (1948): 315–16.

26. *T.L.* is also used commonly as a verb, with inflected forms *T.L.d, T.L.s, T.L.ing,* and the derivative *T.L.er.*

27. L. M. Feinsilver, "Yiddish Idioms in American English," p. 206.

28. *Book Digest,* October 1975, p. 145.

29. *Time,* October 23, 1972, p. 106.

30. William Safire, "The Meese Mess," *New York Times,* March 30, 1984. The title itself is probably a pun on Yiddish *miese mayse* 'ugly affair.'

31. See Leo Spitzer, "Confusion Schmooshun," *Journal of English and Germanic Philology* 51 (1952): 226–33, and L. M. Feinsilver, "On Yiddish Shm-," p. 302.

32. David L. Gold, "Nudnik," *Comments on Etymology* 12 (1982): 19–22.

33. The word was probably well known in American English long before the 1940s. One of Mack Sennett's silent films of the 1920s

was *Nudnik of the North*, a parody of Robert Flaherty's classic documentary, *Nanook of the North* (1922).

34. In *The Joys of Yiddish*, Rosten, using the spelling *nudzh*, defines the noun as an action, such as a kick under the table. I haven't been able to confirm this use; so far as I know a *nudzh* or *noodge* or *nudge* is nothing more than a nudnik. In fact, Rosten himself quotes this use from a 1967 movie in which an actress snaps at a stagestruck adolescent: "Don't be a nudzh!"

35. L. M. Feinsilver, "Who Needs It?" *American Speech* 41 (1966): 270–73.

36. L. M. Feinsilver, *The Taste of Yiddish*, p. 295.

37. David L. Gold, "Breaking One's Head," *American Speech* 58 (1983): 96.

38. Joey L. Dillard, *Perspectives on American English: Contributions to the Sociology of Language* 29, ed. Joshua A. Fishman (The Hague: Mouton, 1980). Unfortunately, many mechanical errors appear in the Feinsilver extract (pp. 206–55), as they do throughout this otherwise excellent book.

Chapter 6

1. H. B. Wells, "Notes on Yiddish," *American Speech* 4 (1928): 66.

2. C. K. Thomas, "Jewish Dialect and New York Dialect," *American Speech* 7 (1932): 321–26.

3. William Labov, *The Social Stratification of English in New York City* (Washington, D.C.: Center for Applied Linguistics, 1966).

4. William Labov, *Sociolinguistic Patterns* (Philadelphia: University of Pennsylvania Press, 1972).

5. George Jochnowitz, "Bilingualism and Dialect Mixture Among Lubavitcher Hasidic Children," *American Speech* 43 (1968): 182–200.

6. Joshua A. Fishman, review of Walt Wolfram, *Sociolinguistic Aspects of Assimilation*, *Language* 51 (1975): 776.

7. David L. Gold, *Jewish Language Review* 2 (1982): 134.

8. Richard N. Levy, review of Raphael Patai, *Tents of Jacob*, *The New York Times Book Review*, January 9, 1972, p. 4.

9. Joshua A. Fishman, "The Sociology of Jewish Languages from the Perspective of the General Sociology of Language: A Preliminary Formulation," *International Journal of the Sociology of Language* 30 (1981): 15.

10. Nathan Süsskind, [Principles for the Study of Jewish Languages], *Yidishe shprakh* 25 (1965): 1–17.

11. J. A. Fishman, "The Sociology of Jewish Languages," p. 15.

12. N. Süsskind, [Principles], p. 8.

13. J. A. Fishman, "The Sociology of Jewish Languages," p. 10.

14. The material that follows was published originally in somewhat different form in my article, "Jewish English in the United States," *American Speech* 56 (1981): 3–16.

15. No exact data exists for the number of Orthodox Jews in the United States. Thirty-five years ago Charles Liebman, in a pioneering sociological study ("Orthodoxy in American Life," *American Jewish Yearbook* [Philadelphia: Jewish Publication Society of America, 1965]) put the number of "committed" Orthodox at approximately 200,000. The subsequent ethnic and religious revival among American Jews infused new blood into Orthodoxy, greatly increasing the numbers of those counting themselves among the Orthodox. In 1976, George Dugan, writing in *The New York Times* of May 28 (p. A16) put the figure of American Orthodox Jews at 1.5 million. In the 1980s, a survey of the Jewish population in the New York City area, conducted by the Federation of Jewish Philanthropies (see *Young Israel Viewpoint*, February 1983, pp. 10–13) gave the number of those who identified themselves as Orthodox as roughly 230,000. Considering that there are close to six million Jews in the United States (Chapter 1, note 9), it is not farfetched to assume that throughout the entire country another 200,000 Jews might identify themselves as Orthodox.

16. S. M. Breslauer, "Yeshiva Education: Reclaiming the Secular Departments," *Jewish Observer*, January 1973, p. 13. This and other excerpts below are quoted as they appeared in the original (without changing the spellings of the Yiddish- and Hebrew-origin words) except for intrusive typographical devices (italics, boldface, capitals, quotation marks) that many Jewish-English writers and editors conventionally use to render what they consider non-English or nonstandard English forms.

17. Both -*ele* and -*nik* were borrowed in Israel from Yiddish and have become fully. established there, being appended ad hoc to countless Modern Hebrew words. Of the Israeli words ending in -*nik* the only one that has entered American English is *kibbutznik*.
18. David L. Gold, "American Eastern Ashkenazic English *Tsimes,*" *Comments on Etymology* 12 (1982): 7–8.
19. I am indebted for this comment to Professor Nathan Süsskind.
20. Data supplied by William Helmreich, Chairman of the Department of Sociology at City College, New York, in the Rabbi I. Usher Kirshblum Lecture Series delivered by Dr. Helmreich, April–May 1984, at Kew Garden Hills, New York.

Conclusion

1. Max Zeldner, "Yiddish: A Living Language," *Jewish Frontier,* April 1974, p. 14. The quarterly *YIDDISH,* mentioned in this article, reached its tenth year of publication in 1983 with a double issue devoted to the Yiddish theater.
2. Elenore Lester, "Yiddish Comes Out of the Shtetl," *The New York Times Magazine,* December 2, 1979, p. 193.
3. Michael Knight, "Yiddish Book Collection Grows in New England," *The New York Times,* February 17, 1981, p. C5.
4. In 1588 an adviser to Queen Elizabeth I prophesied: "Welsh will be dead in a generation!" It is still alive.
5. Eugene Green, *Yiddish and English in Detroit* (Ann Arbor, Mich.: University Microfilms, 1961), p. 108.

Select Bibliography

Birnbaum, Solomon A. "Jewish Languages." *Encyclopaedia Judaica*, vol. 10 (1972): 66–70.

Copeland, Robert M., and Nathan Süsskind, eds. *The Language of Herz's "Esther": A Study of Judeo-German Dialectology*. University: The University of Alabama Press, 1976.

Feinsilver, Lillian Mermin. "Like Influences from Yiddish and Pennsylvania German." *American Speech* 33 (1958): 231–33.

———. "On Yiddish Shm-." *American Speech* 35 (1961): 302–3.

———. "Yiddish Idioms in American English." *American Speech* 37 (1962): 200–6.

———. "Who Needs It?" *American Speech* 41 (1966): 270–73.

———. *The Taste of Yiddish*. New York and London: Thomas Yoseloff, 1970. Reprint ed., San Diego: A. S. Barnes, 1980.

———. "Yiddish *Ganef*: Its Family and Friends." *American Speech* 47 (1975): 147–51.

———. "Yiddish for Fun and Profit." *Verbatim* 10 (1983): 1–3.

Feldstein, Stanley. *The Land That I Show You: Three Centuries of Jewish Life in America*. New York: Anchor Books, 1979.

Fishman, Joshua A. *Yiddish in America: Sociolinguistic Description and Analysis. International Journal of American Linguistics*, vol. 31, No. 2. Indiana University Press, 1965.

———, ed. *Never Say Die: A Thousand Years of Yiddish in Jewish Life and Letters*. The Hague: Mouton, 1981.

———. "The Sociology of Jewish Languages from the Perspective of the General Sociology of Language: A Preliminary Formula-

163

tion." *International Journal of the Sociology of Language* 30 (1981): 5–16.

———. [On Yiddish, Modernization, and Re-ethnification]. *Oyfn shvel* (1982): 1–7.

———. [On the Future of Yiddish]. *Oyfn shvel* (1983): 2–4.

Gold, David L. "Jewish Intralinguistics as a Field of Study." *International Journal of the Sociology of Language* 30 (1981): 31–46.

———. "Recent American Studies in Jewish Languages." *Jewish Language Review* 1 (1981): 11–88.

———. "Etymological Studies of Jewish Interest, Part I." *Comments on Etymology* 12, 5–6 (December 1–15, 1982): 4–48.

———. "Etymological Studies of Jewish Interest, Part II." *Comments on Etymology* 12, 9–10 (February 1–15, 1983): 3–40.

Green, Eugene. *Yiddish and English in Detroit: A Survey and Analysis of Reciprocal Influences in Bilinguals' Pronunciation, Grammar, and Vocabulary.* Ann Arbor, Mich.: University Microfilms, 1961.

Haugen, Einar. *Bilingualism in the Americas: A Bibliography and Research Guide.* Publication of the American Dialect Society No. 26. University: The University of Alabama Press, 1956. Reprinted 1964 and 1968.

———. "Bilingualism, Language Contact, and Immigrant Languages in the United States: A Research Report 1956–1970." In *Current Trends in Linguistics,* vol. 10, ed. Thomas A. Sebeok, 506–91. The Hague: Mouton, 1973.

Heilman, S. C. "Sounds of Modern Orthodoxy: The Language of Talmud Studies." In *Never Say Die: A Thousand Years of Yiddish in Jewish Life and Letters,* ed. Joshua A. Fishman, 227–53. The Hague: Mouton, 1981.

Howe, Irving. *World of Our Fathers: the Journey of the East European Jews to America and the Life They Found and Made.* New York: Harcourt Brace Jovanovich, 1976.

Jochnowitz, George. "Bilingualism and Dialect Mixture Among Lubavitcher Hasidic Children." *American Speech* 43 (1968): 182–200.

Joffe, Judah A. "The Development of Yiddish in the United States." *Universal Jewish Encyclopedia,* vol. 10 (1943): 601–2.

——— and Mark, Yudel. *Groyser verterbukh fun der yidisher*

shprakh [Great Dictionary of the Yiddish Language], 2 vols. New York: Yiddish Dictionary Committee, 1961–66.

Landis, Joseph C. "Yiddish is Alive and Well." *Keeping Posted* 20 (1974): 3–5.

———. "America and Yiddish Literature." *Jewish Book Annual* 33 (1975–76): 20–32.

Mencken, H. L. *The American Language.* New York: Alfred Knopf, 1923 (3rd ed.), 1936 (4th ed.), 1963 (4th ed. and two Supplements, with annotations and new material by Raven I. McDavid, Jr., with the assistance of David W. Maurer).

Patai, Raphael. *Tents of Jacob: The Diaspora—Yesterday and Today.* New Jersey: Prentice-Hall, 1971.

Poll, Solomon. *The Hasidic Community of Williamsburg: A Study in the Sociology of Religion.* New York: Shocken Books, 1962.

———. "The Role of Yiddish in American Ultra-Orthodox and Hasidic Communities." *YIVO Annual of Jewish Social Science* 13 (1965): 125–52.

Rosenbaum, Samuel. *A Yiddish Word Book for English-Speaking People.* New York: Van Nostrand Reinhold Co., 1978.

Rosten, Leo. *The Joys of Yiddish.* New York: McGraw-Hill, 1968.

———. *Hooray for Yiddish!* New York: Simon and Shuster, 1982.

Samuel, Maurice. *In Praise of Yiddish.* New York: Cowles Book Co., 1971.

Strassfeld, Sharon and Michael. *The Jewish Catalog: A Do-It-Yourself Kit* (now usually called *The First Jewish Catalog*). Philadelphia: The Jewish Publication Society of America, 1973.

———. *The Second Jewish Catalog: Sources and Resources.* Philadelphia: The Jewish Publication Society of America, 1976.

———. *The Third Jewish Catalog: Creating Community.* Philadelphia: The Jewish Publication Society of America, 1980.

Stutchkoff, Nahum. *Der oytser fun der yidisher shprakh* [The Thesaurus of the Yiddish Language]. New York: YIVO Institute for Jewish Research, 1950.

Süsskind, Nathan. [Reflections on the History of Yiddish]. *Yidishe shprakh* 13 (1953): 97–98.

———. [Principles for the Study of Jewish Languages]. *Yidishe shprakh* 25 (1965): 1–17.

———. "A Reply to Many Questions: Common Misconceptions

About Language in General and Yiddish in Particular," *Bnai Yiddish* 12 (1970): 10–17.

———. See Copeland.

Weinberg, Bella Hass. *Ambiguities in the Romanization of Yiddish.* New York: YIVO Institute for Jewish Research, 1997.

Weinreich, Max. [On English Elements in Standard Yiddish]. *Yidishe shprakh* (1941): 33–46.

———. "Prehistory and Early History of Yiddish: Facts and Conceptual Framework." In *The Field of Yiddish*, ed. Uriel Weinreich, 73–101. New York: Linguistic Circle of New York, 1954.

———. *History of the Yiddish Language.* Chicago: The University of Chicago Press, 1980. (Translated by Shlomo Noble, with the assistance of Joshua A. Fishman, from the Yiddish original, *Geshikhte fun der yidisher shprakh.* 4 vols. New York: YIVO Institute of Jewish Research, 1973).

Weinreich, Uriel. *College Yiddish.* New York: YIVO Institute for Jewish Research, 1949. Fifth Revised Edition, 1971.

———. *Languages in Contact.* New York: Linguistic Circle of New York, 1953.

———, ed. *The Field of Yiddish.* New York: Linguistic Circle of New York, 1954.

———. *Modern English-Yiddish Yiddish-English Dictionary.* New York: YIVO Institite for Jewish Research, McGraw-Hill Book Co., 1968.

———. "Yiddish Language." *Encyclopaedia Judaica*, vol. 16 (1972): 790–98.

Index

About the Author

Sol Steinmetz is a linguist and lexicographer who was educated at Yeshiva University and Columbia University. He was the general editor of *The World Book Dictionary*, coauthor of *The Barnhart Dictionary of New English* series, and Editor in Chief of the *Random House Webster's College Dictionary*. He has contributed articles to *Encyclopedia Americana, The Oxford Companion to the English Language, American Speech, Comments on Etymology, Jewish Language Review, The New York Times Magazine*, and *Verbatim*. He and his wife reside in New Rochelle, New York.